The process of rearming the German military after the defeat of 1918 had in reality begun in secret before the Treaty of Versailles had been signed. The terms imposed by the victorious Allies drastically restricted the number of full-time personnel and the types of weapons allowed to the Germans but both were circumvented in a number of ingenious ways, often in direct contravention of the agreement (1).

By 1933, and the ascension to power of Hitler and the National Socialists, any pretence that Germany was abiding by the terms of the Treaty was dropped and within two years the firms of Daimler-Benz, Krupp, Maschinenfabrik Augsburg-Nürnberg (MAN) and Rheinmetall-Borsig had been asked to submit plans for light and medium tanks designs. These vehicles were to replace the Pzkpfw I and II light tanks then in service, which were little more than propaganda tools, and be capable of taking on the current, and anticipated future, generations of enemy armoured vehicles. The resulting designs, the Pzkpfw III and IV, were indeed a huge step forward in the development of the main battle tank and were intended to be used in integrated and massed armoured assaults and not seen as an adjunct to the infantry. The lighter vehicle was originally designated as the 37mm Geschütz-Panzerwagen and later renamed Zugführerwagen, or platoon commander's vehicle (2). An important stipulation of the initial specification was that armour was to be provided on all surfaces, reflecting the intention that the tank was to operate in the forward element of any assault and needed to be protected on all sides. The choice of a suitable weapon was the cause of controversy with the Heereswaffenamt, or army ordnance department, believing that a 3.7cm gun was sufficient. The proponents of armoured warfare and the tank commanders themselves argued for the larger 5cm weapon but as the army's main towed anti-tank gun was based on the Rheinmetall 3.7cm L/45, the view of the Heereswaffenamt prevailed (3).

After evaluating the Krupp and Daimler-Benz designs the Heereswaffenamt decided on the latter and the tank was ordered into production in 1937 as the Panzerkampfwagen (Pzkpfw) III. The development prototypes were fitted the 3.7cm main gun and two machine guns and the armour was of 15mm thickness, which was able to withstand any anti-tank rifle then in use. But the design's real advantage lay in running the drive shaft

Notes

1. Somewhat ironically the Soviet Union, the other pariah state of Europe, was to play a large part in helping the Germans in their covert rearmament programme.
2. This should not be confused with the later purpose-built Befehlspanzerwagen III command tank and the name may have been deliberately confusing.
3. The towed gun was at that time being replaced in the Panzerjäger battalions and companies by the 3.7cm Pak 35/36 which was thought to be the latest word in anti-tank weaponry.

I0896513

Pzkpfw III ausf F tanks, identified by the turret ring guard, under construction. Note the earlier style commander's cupola and the cover above the driver's visor. Note also that the hull of the tank being lifted by the cables does have the Sehklappe, or side vision port for the driver on the right-hand side, a feature which usually identifies early Pzkpfw III ausf E models.

A late production Pzkpfw III ausf G or ausf H of Panzergruppe 2 photographed during the early stages of Operation Barbarossa. Although it is not possible to be certain, these tanks may be from II.Abteilung, Panzer-Regiment 6.

under the vehicle floor which allowed for the turret to be placed at the centre of the hull and created room for a five-man crew. Additionally, the entire crew was linked by a radio communication system which allowed orders to be passed efficiently and quickly even in the noise of battle. These were enormous advantages in an era when tank crews were commonly made up of two or three soldiers who were forced to communicate through hand signals. The first variants, designated Pzkpfw III ausf A, B, C and D, were little more than research and development vehicles with just sixty of all types being built. Although a few did take part in the Polish campaign, and a very small number were in service in northern Russia and Finland when Operation Barbarossa began, they will only be mentioned briefly in this book.

The Pzkpfw III ausf E, which went into production in 1938, featured a torsion bar suspension, which had been developed by Porsche, and this arrangement proved so successful that it was used on all future variants and also for the Sturmgeschütz III assault gun. It is in this configuration that the Pzkpfw III will probably be most familiar to readers.

Although a few vehicles had been tested during the battles in Poland, as mentioned earlier, by May 1940, when the German army crossed into Holland, Belgium and France, a total of 381 Pzkpfw III tanks were in service with the Panzer regiments making up 36 percent of the army's fighting tanks (1).

The number of tanks available had in fact dropped to 350 by June 1941 but the importance of the Pzkpfw III design cannot be underestimated and of the seventeen Panzer regiments massed along the eastern border in preparation for Operation Barbarossa, eleven were equipped with this reliable and sturdy vehicle. By this time the more powerful 5cm L/42 gun had been incorporated into production with the introduction of the Pzkpfw III ausf G and ausf J and as older vehicles were returned to the factories for repair they were updated to the most recent standards. These changes are discussed further in the Technical Details & Modifications section of this book.

Operation Barbarossa, the invasion of the Soviet Union, was a massive undertaking and its history could not possibly be covered in detail in a book of this size. However, the timeline on the following pages and the accompanying map will at least give the reader some understanding of the campaign as it affected the Panzer units, and an idea of where the major events took place. I should mention that I have used the terms and dates employed in contemporary or modern Western histories when referring to battles as the Soviet accounts often differ.

Notes

1. I have deliberately not included the 2,169 Pzkpfw I and II tanks which were little more than scouting vehicles by this stage and the 244 largely unarmed Befehlspanzerwagen command tanks.

EASTERN EUROPE
The national borders depicted here are those of late 1939 following the defeat of Poland and the division of its territory between Germany and the USSR.
Estonia, Latvia and Lithuania were all annexed by the Soviet Union in June 1940. Officially Ukraine and Byelorussia were independent Soviet republics but they were in reality controlled by Moscow. With the end of the Second World War in 1945 and the dissolution of the Soviet Union in 1991 the names of many towns and cities were changed and I have endeavoured to use those that readers may be familiar with. The timeline on the following pages gives a brief outline of the Barbarossa campaign until the start of the Soviet offensives of early December 1941.
FINLAND
Helsinki
Lake Ladoga
Gulf of Finland
LENINGRAD (St Petersburg)
Tallinn
Kohta-Järve
Gatchina
ESTONIA
Pärnu
Tartu
Novgorod
Baltic Sea
Ventspils
Pskov
Staraya Russa
Riga
Demyansk
Rybinsk
Jelgava
Ostrov
Kholm
Memel
LATVIA
Kalinin
LITHUANIA
Velikiye Luki
Daugavpils
Rzhev
Königsberg (Kaliningrad)
Kaunus
MOSCOW
Vilna (Vilnius)
Vitebsk
Yartsevo
Vyazma
EAST PRUSSIA
Kolomna
Orsha
Smolensk
Serpukhov
GERMANY
Minsk
BYELORUSSIA
Kaluga
Ryazan
Bialystok
Mogilev
Tula
WARSAW
Baranowicze
Siedlce
Bobriusk
Bryansk
Brest-Litovsk
Klintsy
Orel
Pinsk
Lublin
Gomel
Yelets
Mozyr
POLAND (GENERAL GOVERNMENT)
Kovel
Shostka
Kursk
Lutsk
Voronezh
Jaroslaw
Novohrad-Volynskyi
Nezhin
Konotop
Brody
Zhytomyr
Sumy
Lvov
Kiev
Romny
Belgorod
Ternopol
Berdychiv
Pavlovsk
UKRAINE
Kharkov
Khmelnytskyi
Vinnytsia
Cherkasy
Poltava
Zmie
Kremenchug
Chernovsty
Uman
HUNGARY
Kropyvnytskyi
Dniepropetrovsk
Balta
Pervomaisk
Krivoy Rog (Kryvyi Rih)
Stalino (Donetsk)
Cluj
Jassy
Zaporozhye
Nikopol
Nikolayev
Rostov-on-Don
ROMANIA
Kishinev
Tiraspol
Mariupol
Sibiu
Kherson
Odessa
Brasov
Galatz
Krasnoperekopsk
Miles 50 100
Sea of Azov
Kilometres 50 100
Black Sea
Kerch
Simferopol
Bucharest
Sevastopol

21 June 1941. *The last German troops move into their positions along the western borders of the Soviet Union from Lithuania in the north to Romania in the south. In the early afternoon German army group commanders receive coded messages that confirm the invasion will begin the next day.*

22 June 1941. *At around 3:15 am a devastating artillery barrage pounds the Russian positions along the entire front. As air raids hit targets as far afield as the Soviet naval bases at Kronstadt and Sevastopol, more than 3,000,000 German troops and their Axis allies begin their advance. In what is almost certainly the first use of submersible armoured vehicles, specially-adapted Pzkpfw III and IV tanks cross the River Bug near the Polish village of Pratulin, 20 kilometres north-west of Brest-Litovsk.*

23 June 1941. *Six Soviet mechanised corps, with over 2,500 tanks, prepare to launch a series of counterattacks against the flanks of Panzergruppe 1 between Brody and Lutsk in what is today western Ukraine. Harassed by the Luftwaffe and lacking effective communications the Russians postpone the attack. Elsewhere, on the same day, units of 6.Panzer-Division come into contact with the enemy's KV series of heavy tanks.*

24 June 1941. *At 4:00 am the Russian assault against Panzergruppe 1 finally gets underway but only two Red Army division take part. By the end of the day units of Heeresgruppe Nord have advanced deep into Lithuania and Byelorussia, present-day Belarus. Hitler arrives at his new forward headquarters in East Prussia.*

25 June 1941. *Despite the Russian counterattacks near Brody, units of Panzergruppe 1 capture Dubno and Lutsk. The tanks of 11.Panzer-Division and 16.Panzer-Division have advanced almost 60 kilometres into Soviet territory.*

26 June 1941. *Elements of LVI.Panzerkorps, including 8.Panzer-Division, cross the Western Dvina River in modern-day Belarus and establish a bridgehead in Soviet territory. On the same day Finland formally declares war against the Soviet Union.*

27 June 1941. *German troops capture Bobriusk in Belarus and Przemyel in Soviet-occupied Poland. Early the following day, in what may have been the German army's first encounter with the T-34 tank, the units of 16.Panzer-Division beat off a Russian counterattack near Dubno on the Lutsk to Ternipol road.*

28 June 1941. *German troops capture Minsk, the capital city of modern-day Belarus, encircling the survivors of twenty-seven Soviet army divisions.*

29 June 1941. *On the northern front the Russians begin falling back to the Stalin Line in front of Leningrad, present-day St Petersburg. Finnish and German units, including the tanks of Panzer-Abteilung zbV 40, launch an attack towards Murmansk. The mechanised divisions of Heeresgruppe Mitte, including Panzergruppen 2 and 3, are ordered to stop to allow their supporting infantry formations to catch up.*

30 June 1941. *The Soviet operation near Brody is finally called off. This action, although relatively unknown in the West, was the largest tank battle of the campaign. Tanks of II.Abteilung, Panzer-Regiment 18 capture the bridge over the Berezina River at Borisov, present-day Barysaw in Belarus, after a fierce skirmish.*

1 July 1941. *The tanks of Panzergruppe 4 enter Riga in Latvia while elements of Panzergruppe 2 reach the Berezina River north of Bobriusk in Belarus.*

2 July 1941. *Panzergruppe 4, under Heeresgruppe Nord, begins its attack against the Stalin Line, quickly breaking through near Ostrov. The armoured units of Heeresgruppe Mitte resume their advance but a massive storm brings their progress to a halt. The rain lasts for six days and allow the Russians to build their defences.*

A Pzkpfw III ausf H Tauchpanzer submersible tank of 1.Kompanie, Panzer-Regiment 36 photographed during the invasion of the Soviet Union. Clearly visible are the metal flanges around the gun mantlet and machine-gun aperture, which held the waterproof covers, and the step welded to the hull side. The unit insignia of 14.Panzer-Division can be seen to the right of the driver's visor.

A Pzkpfw III ausf G of 3.Kompanie, Panzer-Abteilung zbV 40 photographed in northern Russia during the summer battles of 1941. This tank has been upgraded by the application of additional armour, or Zusatzpanzerung, on the hull front and the suspension has been reworked to accept the wider Kgs 61/400/120 tracks, although it retains the early drive sprocket and rear idler.

3 July 1941. *The Germans eliminate a large Soviet defensive pocket at Bialystok in eastern Poland claiming the capture of 300,000 Russian soldiers.*

5 July 1941. *Following a breakthrough made by 6.Armee near Lvov, tanks of Panzergruppe 1 push towards Zhytomyr and Berdychiv in central Ukraine.*

6 July 1941. *The Russians launch a major counterattack near Smolensk against the advance of XLVII.Panzerkorps but run into the anti-tank defences of 7.Panzer-Division. In five days of vicious fighting the Germans destroy over 800 Soviet tanks.*

7 July 1941. *German armoured units cross the Western Dvina River and outflank the Polotsk fortifications.*

8 July 1941. *The tanks of Panzergruppe 4, having smashed through the Stalin Line, capture Pskov and enter what are today the outer suburbs of Leningrad.*

9 July 1941. *Panzergruppe 4 begins a series of assaults on the Soviet defensive positions along the Luga River near Leningrad.*

10 July 1941. *Zhytomyr on the Teteriv River in Ukraine falls to 13.Panzer-Division.*

11 July 1941. *Vitebsk, present-day Viciebsk in Belarus, is captured by Panzergruppe 3.*

13 July 1941. *The tanks of 20.Panzer-Division establish a bridgehead on the eastern bank of the Dvina River.*

14 July 1941. *Encouraged by the advances in the East, Hitler orders the arms industry to switch production from guns and tanks to aircraft and submarines.*

15 July 1941. *Kozyatyn, 15 kilometres south-east of Berdychiv, is captured by 16.Panzer-Division. Elements of 7.Panzer-Division and 20.Panzer-Division reach Yartsevo, 40 kilometres east of Smolensk.*

16 July 1941. *Tanks of Panzer-Regiment 29 enter Smolensk on the road to Moscow. Although the city centre is secured, fighting rages in the suburbs for over a week.*

17 July 1941. *Units of Panzergruppe 1 consolidate their positions around Kozyatyn threatening the encirclement of twenty Soviet divisions near Uman in southern Ukraine.*

18 July 1941. *Elements of 16.Panzer-Division cross the Ros River and force the Russians out of their positions at Stavysche, cutting the Uman to Kiev road. Over the next days the Panzers repel several counterattacks.*

19 July 1941. *In a major revision of the Barbarossa plan, Hitler directs that the assault on Moscow will be cancelled and the main effort switched to the destruction of the Russian forces around Kiev. Panzergruppe 2 is to be transferred to Heeresgruppe Nord and Panzergruppe 3 will be subordinated to Heeresgruppe Süd. All his commanders disagree and urge that the capture of the Soviet capital be given priority.*

20 July 1941. *Velikiye Luki, north of Smolensk, is captured by 19.Panzer-Division but retaken by the Soviets on the following day. Elements of 10.Panzer-Division capture Yelnya, south-east of Smolensk.*

21 July 1941. *Soviet troops abandon the defensive positions along the Dniester River in western Ukraine. The tanks of 7.Panzer-Division repulse a huge Soviet counterattack at Yartsevo.*

22 July 1941. *The Luftwaffe attacks Moscow for the first time.*

23 July 1941. *The fortress of Brest-Litovsk in western Belarus falls to the Germans after a month-long siege.*

25 July 1941. *Velikiye Luki falls to the Germans for a second time.*

26 July 1941. *After attempting a breakout, the remnants of three Soviet armies go into captivity at Mogilev in Belarus near the present-day Russian frontier.*

27 July 1941. *The Russian units around Smolensk are cut off and over 300,000 Red Army soldiers surrender. On the same day German troops capture Tallinn in Estonia.*

29 July 1941. *After a week of fighting, the Russians retake Yartsevo only to be forced out again two days later.*

31 July 1941. *Panzergruppe 4 captures Luga, on the Pskov-Leningrad road.*

1 August 1941. *A Soviet rifle division, which had attempted to fight its way through to Uman, is almost completely wiped out by the tanks of 14.Panzer-Division*

2 August 1941. *The encirclement of the Soviet divisions around Uman is complete. The Germans later report that among the prisoners taken were two army, four corps and eleven divisional commanders.*

3 August 1941. *The city of Roslavl falls to the Germans ending the battle of Smolensk. On the following day the tanks of 4.Panzer-Division destroy the last Russian armoured units that had attempted to break out of the Smolensk Pocket.*

4 August 1941. *Following Hitler's personal order, Panzergruppe 3 is transferred to Heeresgruppe Nord and Panzergruppe 2 is subordinated to Heeresgruppe Süd. This leaves Heeresgruppe Mitte with no armoured reserves.*

5 August 1941. *Units of Heeresgruppe Mitte and Heeresgruppe Nord link up north of Smolensk, encircling over 300,000 Russian soldiers.*

7 August 1941. *German and Finnish units capture Kestenga and reach Ukhta, a further 100 kilometres to the south, but large Soviet reinforcements prevent any further advance.*

8 August 1941. *Tanks of Panzergruppe 4 break through the Soviet defences west of Leningrad. The last Russian defenders of the Uman Pocket lay down their arms.*

12 August 1941. *Hitler orders that Panzergruppen 2 and 3 be returned to Generalfeldmarschall von Bock's Heeresgruppe Mitte, which is also to be reinforced with Panzergruppe 4, and the drive on Moscow resumed. Initially Bock and Halder, the Oberkommando des Heeres (OKH) chief of staff, were satisfied with this compromise solution but both soon realised the immense operational difficulties inherent in such a decision.*

15 August 1941. *13.Panzer-Division, supported by SS-Wiking-Division, reaches Kremenchug in central Ukraine.*

16 August 1941. *German units capture the Soviet naval base at Nikolayev on the Black Sea.*

17 August 1941. *German troops capture Narva in Estonia.*

18 August 1941. *German troops establish a bridgehead across the Dnieper River at Zaporizhia in southern Ukraine.*

19 August 1941. *8.Panzer-Division losses forty-two tanks and other armoured vehicles to a single KV-1 platoon near Krasnogvardeysk, modern-day Gatchina, 30 kilometres south of Leningrad.*

20 August 1941. *In an apparent contradiction of his order of 12 August, Hitler informs his generals that the most important objective of Barbarossa is to deprive the Russians of their industrial base. On the following day OKW issues a directive that summarises the Führer's strategy. Priority is to be given to the destruction of Leningrad, the occupation of the Crimea and the Donbass Region and the isolation of the Caucasus oil fields. In addition, Heeresgruppe Mitte was to eliminate the Soviet forces on the central sector and be prepared to repel any counterattacks. Although most commanders expressed their utter dismay, they did so in private and only Halder offered his resignation which was later withdrawn. On the same day tanks of Panzergruppe 1 enter Kherson in the southern Ukraine but fail to prevent the destruction of the Dnieper River bridge by the retreating Russians.*

24 August 1941. *A Soviet counterattack at Staraya Russa south of Lake Ilmen is beaten back. The tanks of 12.Panzer-Division cut the Moscow to Leningrad rail line.*

26 August 1941. *The tanks of Panzer-Regiment 6 capture the bridge over the River Desna at Novgorod, modern-day Novhorod-Severskyi in Ukraine, but a fanatical Russian defence prevents the Germans from exploiting their success. On the northern sector Soviet units retake Velikiye Luki.*

28 August 1941. *Panzergruppe 2 crosses the Desna River between Novhorod-Severskyi and Korop in north-eastern Ukraine.*

29 August 1941. *Soviet troops evacuated the Karelian Isthmus as Finnish forces retake Viipuri in northern Russia. The tanks of 3.Panzer-Division reach Glukhov, modern-day Hlukhiv in Ukraine, about 50 kilometres north-east of Konotop.*

A Panzerbefehlswagen III ausf H of 14.Panzer-Division. Note the additional 30mm armour plates bolted to the hull front. Although this photograph is damaged, a tactical sign denoting a signals unit and a small number 2 are just visible directly below the hull machine-gun aperture to the right of the headlight, suggesting that this vehicle may be from the headquarters of 2.Kompanie, Panzer-Regiment 36.

Unfortunately there are no markings visible which would allow us to identify the unit to which these two Pzkpfw III Tauchpanzer submersible tanks belong. Althogether 160 Pzkpfw III ausf F, G and H models and eight Befehlswagen III tanks were converted and numbers were allocated to five Panzer divisions for Operation Barbarossa and this is discussed further in the Technical Details & Modifications section of this book.

30 August 1941. *The Russians evacuate Vyborg on the Gulf of Finland just 100 kilometres north-west of Leningrad. Finnish troops occupy the city on the same day.*

1 September 1941. *Units of 3. and 4.Panzer-Divisionen manage to fight their way across the Desna River bridge at Novhorod-Severskyi but are reduced to eighty-six operational tanks.*

3 September 1941. *The Kriegstagebuch, or war diary, of 7.Panzer-Division complains that the appearance of Russian KV heavy tanks on the battlefield is sufficient to cause panic among German infantry units.*

6 September 1941. *A Russian counterattack retakes Yelyna south-east of Smolensk.*

7 September 1941. *German infantry units capture Shlisselburg at the mouth of the Neva River completing the encirclement of Leningrad.*

10 September 1941. *Tanks of 3.Panzer-Division take the town of Romny in eastern Ukraine capturing vast stores of food and fuel.*

12 September 1941. *Panzergruppe 1 crosses the Dnieper River between Cherkasy and Kremenchug in central Ukraine.*

13 September 1941. *Tanks of II.Abteilung, Panzer-Regiment 1 occupy an area of the Pulkovo Heights, the last Russian defensive line before Leningrad, but are pushed back later the same day. Halder confides to his diary that the prospect of the campaign continuing into 1942, although unpalatable, is likely.*

14 September 1941. *The first units of 2.Panzer-Division, which had been rebuilt after the Balkan campaign, arrive on the Eastern Front at Roslavl.*

16 September 1941. *Parts of forty-three Soviet divisions are encircled near Kiev in modern-day Ukraine. After a ten-day battle the Germans claimed to have killed or captured over 400,000 Russian troops. After almost two months of intense combat some German units report personnel and equipment shortfalls of up to 75 percent.*

17 September 1941. *The commander of 3.Panzer-Division, Generalleutnant Walter Model, reports that just 20 percent of his tanks are operational.*

18 September 1941. *Panzergruppe 4 is transferred from Heeresgruppe Mitte in preparation for the drive on Moscow. German troops enter Poltava on the road to Kharkov.*

20 September 1941. *German units are within 10 kilometres of Leningrad.*

23 September 1941. *The German high command, at Hitler's instigation, calls off the assault on Leningrad, deciding to starve the city into submission.*

26 September 1941. *The last defenders of Kiev surrender. The German high command estimates that the Red Army has suffered over 1,000,000 casualties since the start of Operation Barbarossa.*

30 September 1941. *Panzergruppe 4 reaches Uritzk, today a suburb of St Petersburg.*

1 October 1941. *Advancing into the Donbass Region, units of Panzergruppe 1 encircle and destroy two Russian armies.*

2 October 1941. *Heeresgruppe Mitte launches Operation Typhoon, the drive to take Moscow.*

3 October 1941. *The tanks of Panzergruppe 2 enter Orel, north of Kursk on the road between Kharkov and Moscow, and three days later take Bryansk, a further 50 kilometres to the north-west.*

5 October 1941. *Panzergruppe 2 is renamed 2.Panzerarmee.*

7 October 1941. *The first snowfalls are reported on the central sector of the Eastern Front. Within days the snow melts, turning the roads into quagmires.*

10 October 1941. *Lead units of Panzergruppe 3 and Panzergruppe 4 meet up at Vyazma, halfway between Smolensk and Moscow, encircling four Soviet armies.*

***13 October 1941.** German units reach the Mozhaisk Line, a series of defence works west of Moscow stretching from Kalinin and Volokolamsk to Kaluga. The Germans outflank the Russian defences and although they reach Tula, 50 kilometres to the south-east of Kaluga, the Red Army garrison is able to hold the town.*

***16 October 1941.** Panic grips the civilian population of Moscow who attempt to flee, bringing train travel to a complete halt.*

***17 October 1941.** Tanks of 14.Panzer-Division cross the Mius River and take Taganrog on the Black Sea.*

***18 October 1941.** In front of Moscow the Germans take Mozhaisk and Maloyaroslavets, integral parts of the Soviet defensive line.*

***21 October 1941.** Late in the evening, Panzergruppe 1 captures Stalino, modern-day Donetsk, just 100 kilometres from the Black Sea coast.*

***22 October 1941.** The first German units fight their way into Kharkov in eastern Ukraine.*

***24 October 1941.** Kharkov, one of the largest industrial centres of the Soviet Union, falls to the Germans.*

***25 October 1941.** Panzergruppe 1 is renamed 1.Panzerarmee.*

***26 October 1941.** Pushing past the Russian defences, 2.Panzerarmee captures Kalinin and Kaluga, south-west of Moscow, but once again the Germans are held up outside Tula.*

***27 October 1941.** Russian units defending the approaches to Moscow fall back to the Nara River, less than 50 kilometres from the city centre.*

***29 October 1941.** The divisions of 2.Panzerarmee attempt to take Tula but are in such a depleted state that the tanks are halted by a force made up largely of civilian volunteers.*

***31 October 1941.** Confronted by a sea of mud, Oberkommado der Wehrmacht (OKW) orders a temporary halt to all offensive operations in the hope that the approaching cold weather will at least harden the surface of the roads.*

***15 November 1941.** Three German corps, including Panzergruppe 3, strike towards the Volga reservoir and the Moscow Canal in an assault that signals the resumption of Operation Barbarossa.*

***18 November 1941.** Elements of 2.Panzerarmee attempt to complete the encirclement of Moscow but are unsuccessful.*

***19 November 1941.** The tanks of Panzergruppe 3 smash into the flank of the Russian forces at Zvenigorod, 40 kilometres west of Moscow.*

***21 November 1941.** Rostov-on-Don falls to the Germans.*

***22 November 1941.** Although badly under strength, 2.Panzerarmee captures Stalinogorsk, present-day Novomoskovsk east of Tula, surrounding a Soviet rifle division.*

***23 November 1941.** Panzergruppe 3 captures Klin, 85 kilometres north of Moscow, and advances a further 20 kilometres to Solnechnogorsk on the following day.*

***24 November 1941.** Kashira, on the Oka River about 80 kilometres to the south of Moscow, falls to 17.Panzer-Division which almost completely destroys a Soviet army in the process and forces the Russians to commit their last reserves in this area.*

***27 November 1941.** Panzer-Regiment 25, by now reduced to thirty-six operational tanks, manages to establish a bridgehead on the eastern bank of the Volga River at Yakhroma, about 50 kilometres north of Moscow.*

***28 November 1941.** Kampfgruppe Eberbach, made up from the remaining tanks of 3. and 4.Panzer-Divisionen, strike at the Russian defences north of Tula. The Russians retake Rostov-on-Don.*

***30 November 1941.** Generalfeldmarschall von Bock reports to Berlin that his divisions are being asked to operate in temperatures of minus 45 degrees Celsius.*

***1 December 1941.** A German attack along the Minsk-Moscow highway is stalled and then beaten back.*

***2 December 1941.** A German reconnaissance unit secures the bridge over the Moscow Canal at Khimki, just 8 kilometres for the city centre. This is the closest that Axis units will come to the Soviet capital and three days later the Red Army launches a massive counterattack which is able to push the Germans back some 200 kilometres by the first week of the new year. Operation Barbarossa has come to an end.*

A Panzerbefehlswagen III ausf H of Stab, Panzer-Brigade 18. The other command tank operated by this unit is shown on page 24 of the Camouflage & Markings section. Panzer-Division 18 was one of three formations involved in the invasion of the Soviet Union which retained the Panzer brigade headquarters after the armoured divisions were reduced to a single Panzer regiment. This tank is one of justNote the large white letter G on the front of the motorcycle side car identifying Panzergruppe 2, commanded by Generaloberst Heinz Guderian.

GERMAN PANZER UNITS IN THE EAST, JUNE 1941

The diagram below shows the armoured units and their reported strengths as at 21 June 1941, the day before Operation Barbarossa began. Note that this chart only includes German units and that infantry, motorised infantry and other formations are not listed. Oberkommando des Heeres (OKH) was the high command of the army and the post was held by Generalfeldmarschall Walther von Brauchitsch until 19 December 1941 when Hitler took personal control. Serving under OKH was the Chef des Generalstabes des Heeres, the Chief of the General Staff, Generaloberst Franz Halder.

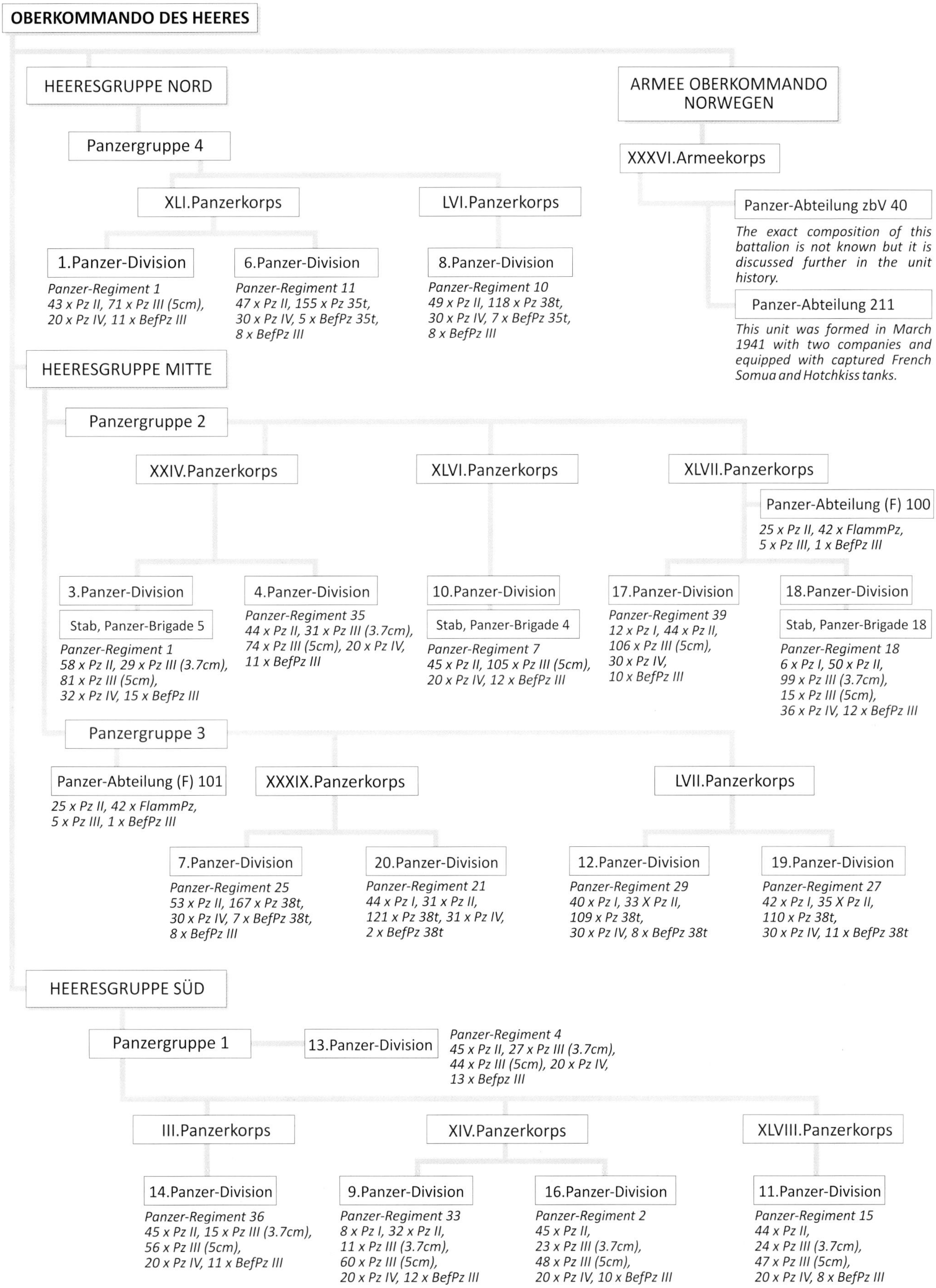

Photographed on 19 August 1941 south of Dniepropetrovsk these Panzerbefehlswagen III command tanks are from the headquarters of Panzer-Regiment 36, 14.Panzer-Division. Note that both have field-modified racks holding jerry cans, of different sizes but similar construction, on the hull side.

A Pzkpfw III, possibly an ausf J model, of 4.Kompanie, Panzer-Regiment 36 photographed at the same time as the tanks shown in the photograph above.

PANZER-REGIMENT, 1941

The Panzer divisions were large and complex formations that underwent numerous organisational changes between 1935, when the first division was created, and 1945 when the war ended. Generally speaking, the first divisions, which took part in the Polish campaign of late 1939, contained two Panzer regiments controlled by a brigade headquarters or Stab. This establishment proved rather unwieldy and although it was retained for the original units into 1940, the new divisions that had been formed for the invasion of France and the Low Countries were built around a single tank regiment consisting of, in most cases, three battalions. In preparation for Operation Barbarossa ten new Panzer divisions were created and these were formed with a single Panzer regiment although some contained just two battalions. The battalions were usually made up of one medium, or Mittlere, company and two light, or Leichte, companies but some contained four companies and details of the organisation and equipment of the regiments that were involved in the initial battles in the Soviet Union are given in the unit histories on the following pages. All units of the German army were organised using charts referred to as Kriegsstärkenachweisungen, abbreviated to KstN, and in February 1941 orders were issued for the reorganisation of the Panzer regiments. These were referred to at the time as Sonder, or special, KstN and are shown in the table below. It should be noted that the new organisation was not substantially different to the previous establishment, particularly in regard to equipment, and the major changes were in the numbers of personnel.

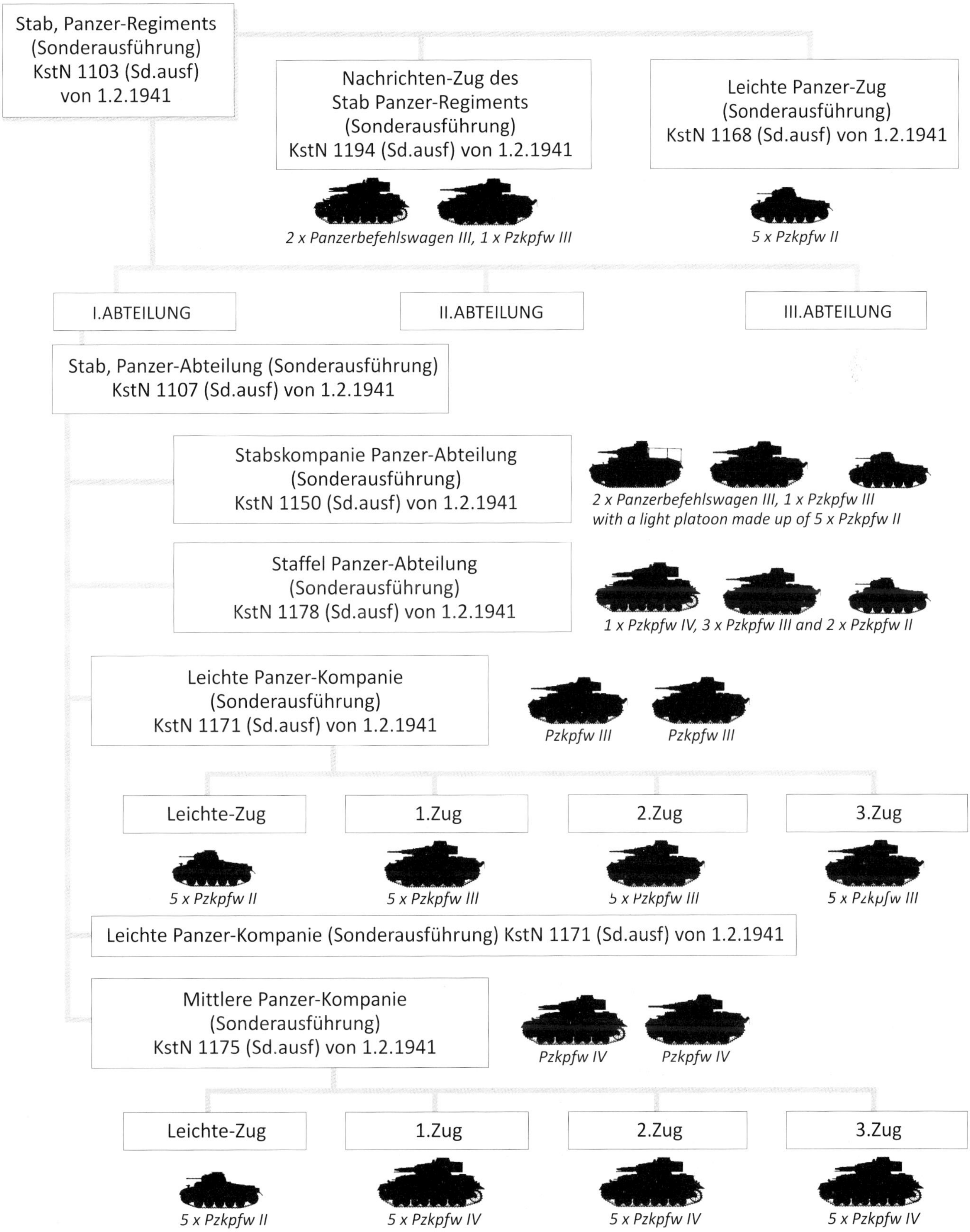

At the commencement of Operation Barbarossa, on 22 June 1941, the German army in the East contained seventeen Panzer divisions and four independent Panzer battalions allocated to four Panzergruppen which were essentially army-sized formations. The affiliations of the divisions at the start of the campaign are shown in the table on page 9.

Panzergruppe 1 was commanded by Generaloberst Ewald von Kleist and contained five of the Panzer divisions, each with a regiment of two battalions (1). In addition, Panzer-Regiment 36 of 14.Panzer-Division was allocated a number of Tauchpanzer submersible tanks. A large number, probably the majority, of Pzkpfw III tanks with these regiments were armed with the 3.7cm gun although a programme to replace these with the 5cm weapon had been underway for some time (2). Panzer-Regiment 33 of 9.Panzer-Division had served in the Balkan campaign and in early June 1941, just before the invasion began, reported that thirty-eight of the regiment's Pzkpfw III tanks were in short or long-term repair. Of the thirty-four replacements that the regiment received at this time, eleven were upgraded versions of early production models. Panzergruppe 1 was renamed 1.Panzerarmee on 25 October 1941.

Panzergruppe 2 was the strongest of all the German armoured formations that took part in Operation Barbarossa. Led by Generaloberst Heinz Guderian, one of the best-known commanders of the Second World War and an early advocate of armoured warfare, Panzergruppe 2 was made up of five divisions, three of which contained regiments of three full battalions. The regiments of the remaining two divisions, 4.Panzer-Division and 10.Panzer-Division, contained six companies of Pzkpfw III tanks which made them approximately the same size. The Panzer regiments of 18.Panzer-Division and 3.Panzer-Division both had a number of Tauchpanzer submersible tanks. Panzergruppe 2 was briefly referred to as Armeegruppe Guderian in late July 1941 and on 5 October was officially renamed 2.Panzerarmee.

All four divisions of Generaloberst Hermann Hoth's Panzergruppe 3 were equipped with Pzkpfw 38t light tanks which had been appropriated by the Germans with the annexation of Czechoslovakia. Only 7.Panzer-Division, of the four divisions available to Generaloberst Hoth, was made up of combat veterans and it was in addition the strongest formation of Panzergruppe 3, with nine light and three medium companies. This formation is sometimes referred to as Panzergruppe Hoth.

Panzergruppe 4, commanded by Generaloberst Erich Hoepner, was the weakest of the German armoured formations and was made up of three Panzer divisions. Although all the Pzkpfw III tanks of 1.Panzer-Division were newer models with the 5cm gun, the battalions of 8.Panzer-Division were equipped with

Although it is not possible to identify the unit to which this early production Pzkpfw III ausf H belongs, the field-modified turret stowage bin is very similar to those seen on tanks of Panzer-Regiment 1.

Notes

1. All the ranks given in this narrative are those that were held at the time the events described took place. As many readers will know, Kleist was later promoted to Generalfeldmarschall.
2. This is discussed further in the Technical Details & Modifications section.

Our photograph shows an Sdkfz 9 heavy halftrack towing a Pzkpfw III ausf H during the summer of 1941. The white letter K on the rear of the halftrack identifies this as Panzergruppe 1 and several features on the turret of the tank, including the large bracket behind the gun mantlet and the inflatable ring around the lower edge, show that is a Tauchpanzer conversion. Of the units attached to Panzergruppe 1, both Panzer-Regiment 2 and Panzer-Regiment 36 had a number of these vehicles on hand but unfortunately this image is not clear enough for a positive identification.

Pzkpfw 38t Czech vehicles and the light companies of Panzer-Regiment 11 of 6.Panzer-Division were fitted out with Pzkpfw 35t light tanks.

Following are brief histories of the Panzer units that took part in the fighting in Poland, the Baltic States and the Soviet Union in 1941. For reasons of space I have deliberately omitted the divisions and regiments that were primarily equipped with Czech-built Pzkpfw 35t and Pzkpfw 38t light tanks.

1.Panzer-Division. Formed in 1935 from parts of 3.Kavallerie-Division, this unit took part in the Polish and French campaigns. Prior to the invasion of the Soviet Union the division was reduced to a single armoured regiment, Panzer-Regiment 1, which was made up of two battalions. Each battalion contained two light companies, equipped with Pzkpfw III tanks, and one medium company. The regiment was commanded by Oberstleutnant Arthur Kopp who had served in armoured units since 1936.

On 22 June 1941 the division was attached to Panzergruppe 4, part of Heeresgruppe Nord, and took part in the tank battle at Raseiniai in Lithuania and later fought at the Dvina River bridgehead near Jekabils in Latvia. In mid-July elements of the regiment reached Luga, a small town about 80 kilometres south of Gatchina and after three weeks of heavy fighting managed to cut the railway line to Leningrad, modern-day St Petersburg, by capturing Moloskovitsy, further to the north-east.

By 9 September 1941, the division was fighting in Pulkovo, today a suburb of St Petersburg, and on the following day reported that of the Pzkpfw III tanks that began the campaign, a total of forty-three were serviceable while thirteen were in repair and fifteen had been completely destroyed. By the middle of the month Panzergruppe 4 was withdrawn from the front line and transferred to Heeresgruppe Mitte in preparation for the drive on Moscow.

On 2 October, as part of Panzergruppe Hoth, the division was employed on the left wing of the German attack and within ten days had seized a crossing of the Volga River at Kalinin, present-day Tver. In November the remnants of the division, by now reduced to a Kampfgruppe of two tank companies and an armoured infantry company, took part in an attack towards Moscow along the Tver to Kiln road, north of the city, coming within 20 kilometres of the Soviet capital. By the end of 1941 the division was engaged in the defensive fighting between Rzhev and Sychyovka over 230 kilometres west of Moscow.

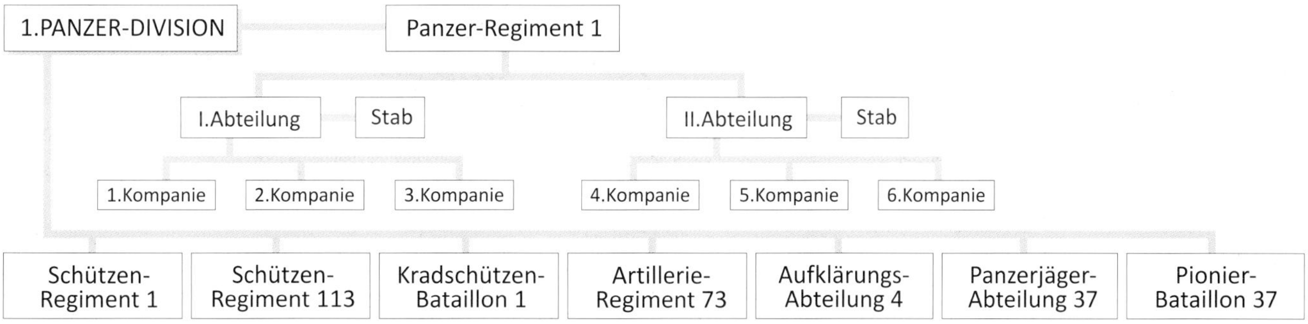

Schützen regiments were renamed as Panzergrenadier in 1942. Service units, such as medical and supply companies, were all numbered 81. Attached to the division was schwere Infanterie-Geschütz-Kompanie 702.

2.Panzer-Division. Formed in 1935, the division originally contained a full tank brigade made up of Panzer-Regiment 3 and Panzer-Regiment 4. In late 1940, following the defeat of France, Panzer-Regiment 4 was permanently detached (1) and the division was reorganised with a single Panzer regiment made up of two battalions. Although the brigade headquarters was retained for some time, by July 1941 it had been disbanded.

The tanks of Panzer-Regiment 3 took part in the fighting in the Balkans and Greece, supporting the mountain infantry of 6.Gebirgs-Division in the capture of Athens. With the conclusion of the fighting in Greece it was planned to return the 2.Panzer-Division to Germany via Italy but on the night of 21 May 1941 many of the division's tracked vehicles were lost when the ships carrying them were sunk. This delayed any future deployment and when Operation Barbarossa commenced the division was refitting in Poland and was later stationed near Bordeaux in France. Assigned to Panzergruppe 4, the first elements of the division arrived on the Eastern Front on 14 September 1941 and the tanks of Panzer-Regiment 3, under the command of Oberst Karl Decker, took part in the fighting around Roslavl, south of Smolensk, and then at Vyazma and Gzhatsk, present-day Gagarin to the west of Moscow. At this time Panzer-Regiment 3 reported that 105 Pzkpfw III and twenty Pzkpfw IV tanks were on hand and from these numbers it would seem that some of the lighter tanks were allocated to the medium companies.

On 15 November, after an enforced halt due to the weather, the German offensive resumed and the division was able to secure Istra and Solnechnogorsk on the Klin to Moscow road, north of the capital, but this was the furthest the tanks would advance. In early December the massive Soviet counterattack drove the survivors of 2.Panzer-Division back the area around Rusa and Volokolamsk, between Moscow and Rzhev.

Notes

1. See 13.Panzer-Division.

- 2.PANZER-DIVISION
  - Panzer-Regiment 3
    - I.Abteilung — Stab
      - 1.Kompanie
      - 2.Kompanie
      - 3.Kompanie
      - 4.Kompanie
    - II.Abteilung — Stab
      - 5.Kompanie
      - 6.Kompanie
      - 7.Kompanie
      - 8.Kompanie
  - Schützen-Regiment 2
  - Schützen-Regiment 304
  - Kradschützen-Bataillon 2
  - Artillerie-Regiment 74
  - Aufklärungs-Abteilung 5
  - Panzerjäger-Abteilung 38
  - Pionier-Bataillon 38

Schützen regiments were renamed as Panzergrenadier in 1942. Service units, such as medical and supply companies, were all numbered 82. Also attached to the division was schwere Infanterie-Geschütz-Kompanie 703.

An upgraded Pzkpfw III ausf F or ausf G of I.Abteilung, Panzer-Regiment 3 photographed in Russia during the summer of 1941. The tank's company number, just behind the good luck horseshoe, appears to begin with either a 2 or 3. The hornet unit insignia on the turret side is one of the variations discussed on page 19 of the Camouflage & Markings section.

3. Panzer-Division. Formed in 1935, the division originally contained Panzer-Regiment 5 and Panzer-Regiment 6 until January 1941 when the latter was permanently detached and sent to North Africa.

Following the French campaign of 1940, the Panzer divisions were all reduced to a single Panzer regiment but some, including 3.Panzer-Division, retained the brigade headquarters. During the 1941 battles in the East these staff formations were used to command ad-hoc battle groups and from October 1941 to January 1942 the division's Panzer-Brigade 5 staff controlled a Kampfgruppe made up from elements of 3.Panzer-Division and 4.Panzer-Division.

At the commencement of Operation Barbarossa Panzer-Regiment 6, commanded by Oberstleutnant Werner von Lewinski März, contained six light companies and the regiment was equipped with a total of 110 Pzkpfw III tanks, although twenty-nine of these were still armed with the 3.7cm gun. As part of Panzergruppe 2, the division took part in the battles east of Brest-Litovsk and then at Bialystok and Minsk, crossing the Berezina River at the end of June near Bobruisk. Within a week the tanks had reached the Dnieper and broken through the Stalin Line. In late August and early September 3.Panzer-Division participated in the fighting around Smolensk and Roslavl and the huge encirclement battle of Kiev and at this time the division reported that just six of the Pzkpfw III tanks that had started the campaign were considered serviceable. As no replacements had been received, this number represented approximately half the division's fighting tanks, the rest being unarmed command tanks and light Pzkpfw I and II vehicles.

After the engagements at Bryansk and Vyazma the tanks of 3.Panzer-Division took part in Operation Typhoon, the assault on Moscow, and captured Tula, on the Moscow to Oryol road, while some forward elements reached Ryazan and Kashira, some 80 kilometres closer to the Soviet capital. Following the Russian counteroffensive the division was pushed back as far as Livny to almost the same positions it had started from in September.

- 3.PANZER-DIVISION
  - Stab, Panzer-Brigade 5
  - Panzer-Regiment 6
    - I.Abteilung – Stab
      - 1.Kompanie, 2.Kompanie, 3.Kompanie
    - II.Abteilung – Stab
      - 4.Kompanie, 5.Kompanie, 6.Kompanie
    - III.Abteilung – Stab
      - 7.Kompanie, 8.Kompanie, 9.Kompanie
  - Schützen-Regiment 3
  - Schützen-Regiment 394
  - Kradschützen-Bataillon 3
  - Artillerie-Regiment 75
  - Aufklärungs-Abteilung 3
  - Panzerjäger-Abteilung 543
  - Pionier-Bataillon 39

Schützen regiments were renamed as Panzergrenadier in 1942. Service units, such as medical and supply companies, were all numbered 83.

A late production Pzkpfw III ausf G from one of the Panzer divisions attached to Panzergruppe 2, identified by the white letter G on the right side fender, photographed during the early weeks of the campaign. The prominent ventilator on the turret roof was indicative of these later vehicles.

The officer seated on the motorcycle is Hans-Detloff von Cossel and this photograph was probably taken at some time after August 1941 when he was promoted to Major and placed in command of I.Abteilung, Panzer-Regiment 35, the regiment's first battalion. The tank in the background is a late production Pzkpfw III ausf G of the regiment's 2.Kompanie. Note the distinctive unit insignia of a standing bear and the wooden beam which was a common feature of the regiment's

- 4.PANZER-DIVISION
  - Panzer-Regiment 35
    - I.Abteilung
      - Stab
      - 1.Kompanie
      - 2.Kompanie
      - 3.Kompanie
      - 4.Kompanie
    - II.Abteilung
      - Stab
      - 5.Kompanie
      - 6.Kompanie
      - 7.Kompanie
      - 8.Kompanie
  - Schützen-Regiment 12
  - Schützen-Regiment 33
  - Kradschützen-Bataillon 34
  - Artillerie-Regiment 103
  - Aufklärungs-Abteilung 7
  - Panzerjäger-Abteilung 49
  - Pionier-Bataillon 79

Schützen regiments were renamed as Panzergrenadier in 1942. Service units, such as medical and supply companies, were all numbered 84.

4.Panzer-Division. Formed in 1938, the division took part in the fighting in Poland and France and during the invasion of the Soviet Union was part of Panzergruppe 2.

The division's Panzer-Regiment 35 was made up of two battalions each containing one medium and three light companies. At that time, thirty-one of the regiment's Pzkpfw III tanks were still armed with the 3.7cm gun while the remaining seventy-four had the 5cm weapon.

During the first weeks of the invasion 4.Panzer-Division took part in the battles at Gomel and Smolensk before being diverted toward the south to support 3.Panzer-Division in the massive encirclement operation around Kiev. On 9 September 1941 the division reported that of the 105 Pzkpfw III tanks that had started the campaign just twenty-four were available for deployment, although fifty-nine were in repair and expected to return at some time.

In early October 1941 the division formed the spearhead of Panzergruppe 2 during the drive on Moscow and captured Orel, modern-day Oryol, after a record advance of 200 kilometres in less than two days through heavy forest.

The OKW situation map for 1 December 1941 shows the division, which must have been reduced to a handful of tanks by that time, holding a bulge in the front line between Metrostroyevskiy and Venyov, about 180 kilometres south of Moscow. Within a few days the Russian counter offensive began and all the German units in this area were driven back.

...........*continued on page 49*

2

1

1. Pzkpfw III ausf H. Panzer-Regiment 1. Baltic States, summer 1941. This vehicle was built by MAN in January 1941 and the Fahrgestellnummer (Fgst Nr), 66150, is just visible in the original image, painted onto the toolbox on the front fender. The improvised stowage bin was typical of this regiment as was the placement of the Balkenkreuz national insignia. I cannot offer any explantion as to the significance of the two dots on the stowage bin although they are quite clear in our photograph. Note that although this tank has the later drive sprocket and rear idler, it is fitted with the earlier pattern shock absorbers. The division's unit insignia (2) was usually carried on the hull front and rear.

3. Pzkpfw III ausf F. Stab, I.Abteilung, Panzer-Regiment 1. Russia, summer 1941. From August 1940 a number of earlier production models were upgraded to the standard of the Pzkpfw III ausf H and it was anticipated that 600 would be ready for Operation Barbarossa. This tank has been partly reworked by the addition of the 5cm gun and additional armour fixed to the hull front (4) although it does not have the later suspension or the so-called Tropen ventilation system.

4

Above: The distinctive Zusatzpanzerung, or hull frontal armour, fitted to Panzer III tanks upgraded as part of the 1940 Umbewaffnung programme. These upgrades are discussed further in the Technical Details & Modifications section of this book.

3

4

1

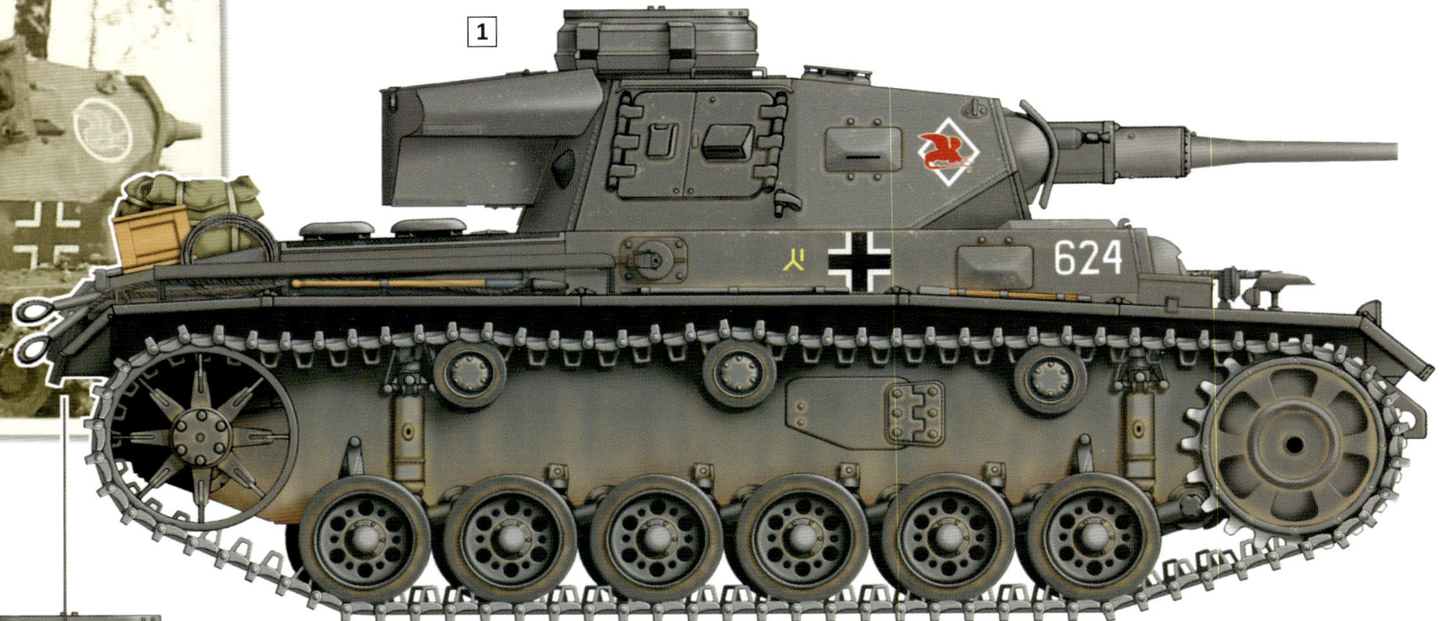

2

3

5

1. Pzkpfw III ausf J. 6.Kompanie, Panzer-Regiment 3. Russia, autumn 1941. Largely re-equipped after the fighting in the Balkans, the regiment did not arrive in the East until September 1941 when the drive towards Moscow was underway. The tanks of II.Abteilung were identified by the colourful insignia shown here made up of a stylised red hornet. The background indicated the platoon with a circle (4), a diamond (1) and a triangle (3) denoting the first, second and third platoons respectively, while the headquarters used a shield (2). It would seem that variations of these designs were later adopted by at least some of the other companies

5. Pzkpfw III ausf J. 6.Kompanie, Panzer-Regiment 3. Russia, autumn 1941. The unit insignia of 2.Panzer-Division was carried on the hull sides, as shown here, and also at the front and rear. The use of the Panzer rhomboid symbol, denoting a tank company, and the company number is less often seen. The Hakenkreuz flag covering the stowage box on the hull rear was commonly used as an aerial recognition device at this stage of the campaign.

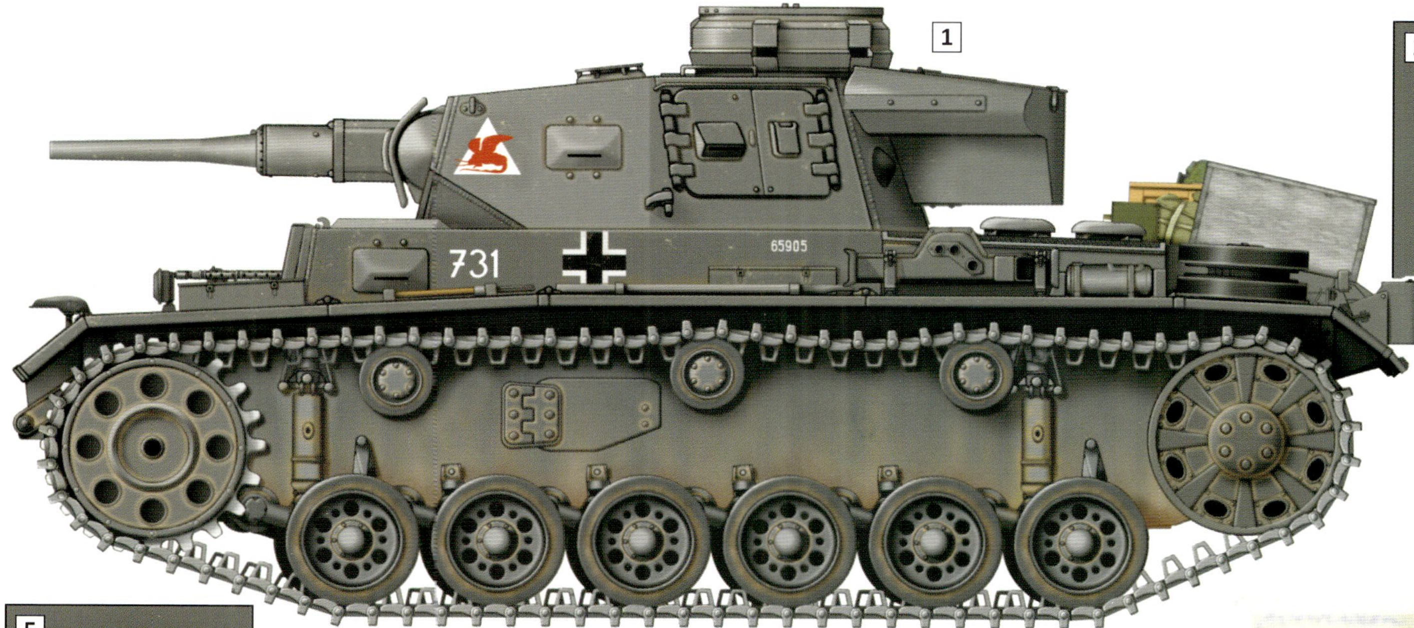

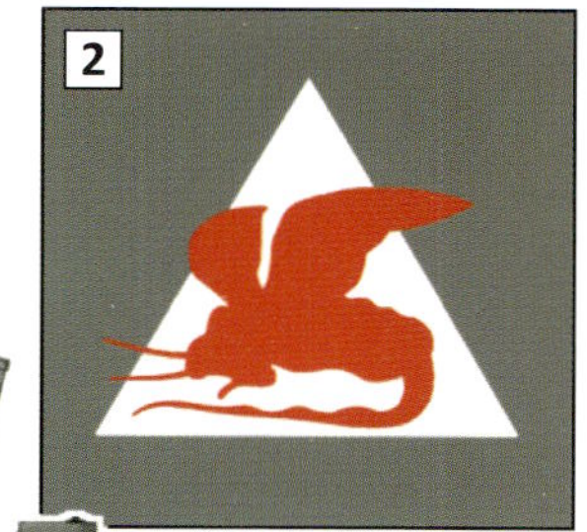

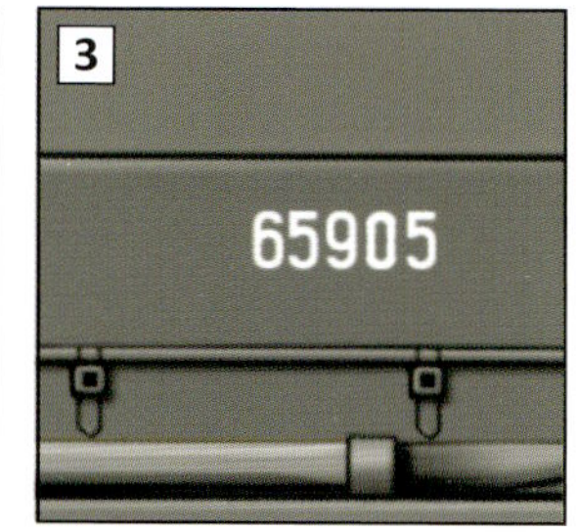

1. Pzkpfw III ausf G. 7.Kompanie, Panzer-Regiment 3. Russia, autumn 1941. This tank, Fgst Nr. 65905, was one of the first Pzkpfw III ausf G tanks completed by MAN in August or September 1940. Note the variation on the unit insignia (2) used by 6.Kompanie and the Fgst number (3) painted on the hull side above the toolbox.

4. Pzkpfw III ausf G. 5.Kompanie, Panzer-Regiment 3. Russia, autumn 1941. The turret stowage bin, or Rommelkiste, was retrofitted to these earlier model tanks and required the metal bracket shown here to hold it in place. Note that the 2.Panzer-Division unit insignia (5) is depicted here in black and is just visible in our photograph (6) on the hull glacis.

1

1. Pzkpfw III. 7.Kompanie, Panzer-Regiment 4. Russia, summer 1941. Although this tank is usually identified as a Pzkpfw III ausf H it is fitted with the wheels and shock absorbers that were used for earlier models and does not have the distinctive Tropen ventilation system. The hull glacis is obscured by lengths of spare track in the photograph on which this illustration is based and this vehicle may be a Pzkpfw III ausf G that was upgraded as part of the Umbewaffnung programme. Apparently the companies of II.Abteilung were numbered as 7, 8 and 9 until April 1942. The unit insignia of 13.Panzer-Division, to which this regiment was attached, is painted onto the hull side in front of the Balkenkreuz.

2

2. Pzkpfw III ausf H. 5.Kompanie, Panzer-Regiment 6. Russia, summer 1941. Although the large turret numbers shown here were commonly seen during the French campaign of 1940, most had been replaced by less conspicuous versions as early as the invasion of the Balkans and Greece. The unit insignia of 3.Panzer-Division (3) can be seen in our photograph (4) painted onto the hull glacis. Note the black outline of the Balkenkreuz.

3

1

2

4

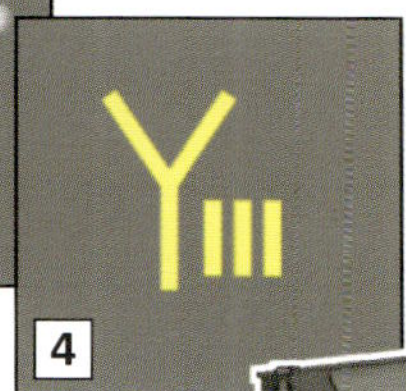

5

1. Pzkpfw III ausf H. 6.Kompanie, Panzer-Regiment 7. Russia, autumn 1941. The standing buffalo insignia of this regiment (2) was probably adopted just before the commencement of the invasion of France and the Low Countries in May 1940 and its use may have eventually been extended to other units of 10.Panzer-Division. It was applied with varying degrees of care, as can be seen in our photograph (3), and was sometimes depicted in black. Note the 10.Panzer-Division formation sign (4) at the hull front and the large stowage box which carries the Balkenkreuz and the tank's number in white on a black panzer rhomboid.

5. Pzkpfw III ausf J. 6.Kompanie, Panzer-Regiment 7. Russia, summer 1941. Although the exact significance of the large white turret numbers is not certain, they may identified the platoons which could have been numbered consecutively throughout the company. The pennant may have identified the platoon commander but its red colour, although entirely possible, is completely speculative on my part.

3

2

1

1. Pzkpfw III ausf H. 1.Kompanie, Panzer-Regiment 15. Russia, summer 1941. In preparation for the invasion of the Soviet union most units fitted their tanks with some form of field-modified stowage bins. The type shown here is commonly seen on tanks of Panzer-Regiment 15, although it was not universal and almost all varied in small details. The white Panzer rhomboid shape denoted a tank of 1.Kompanie and the regiment's famous unit insignia (2) was carried by most tanks in the position shown in our photograph (3), although it could also face towards the left. The letter K, which identifies a unit of Panzergruppe 1, was sometimes repeated on the turret sides.

4

4. Pzkpfw III ausf G. 1.Kompanie, Panzer-Regiment 15. Russia, summer 1941. The tanks were numbered consecutively throughout the company and the numbers were repeated on the turret stowage box. The Gespentser unit insignia (5) may have originally been restricted to the tanks of Panzer-Regiment 15 but it was certainly in use by other units of 11.Panzer-Division in June 1941. The division's official formation sign (6) was also in common use.

5

6

1. Panzerbefehlswagen III ausf H. Stab, I.Abteilung, Panzer-Regiment 18. Ukraine, summer 1941. This unit was trained to take part in the invasion of Britain and the regiment's insignia reflects the amphibious nature of its intended role. Made up of a Panzer Totenkopf above a series of waves on a black shield, a number of variations existed. In fact, I have been unable to find two identical designs although I have been able to examine several photographs. The regiment contained three battalions and just prior to the start of Operation Barbarossa the seventh, eighth and ninth companies were renumbered as 9, 10 and 11 respectively. The identification of this tank with the regiment's first battalion is based on a photograph of Major von Zeschau, the commander of III.Abteilung, in the cupola of his Befehlspanzer which is numbered 30.

2. Pzkpfw III ausf G Tauchpanzer. 11.Kompanie, Panzer-Regiment 18. Ukraine, summer 1941. The turret number identifies the company and, in this case, the individual tank. Note that the number is repeated on the Rommelkiste stowage box (3) and this seems to have been consistent throughout the regiment. Note also the cover for the spare wheel marked with a Balkenkreuz (4).

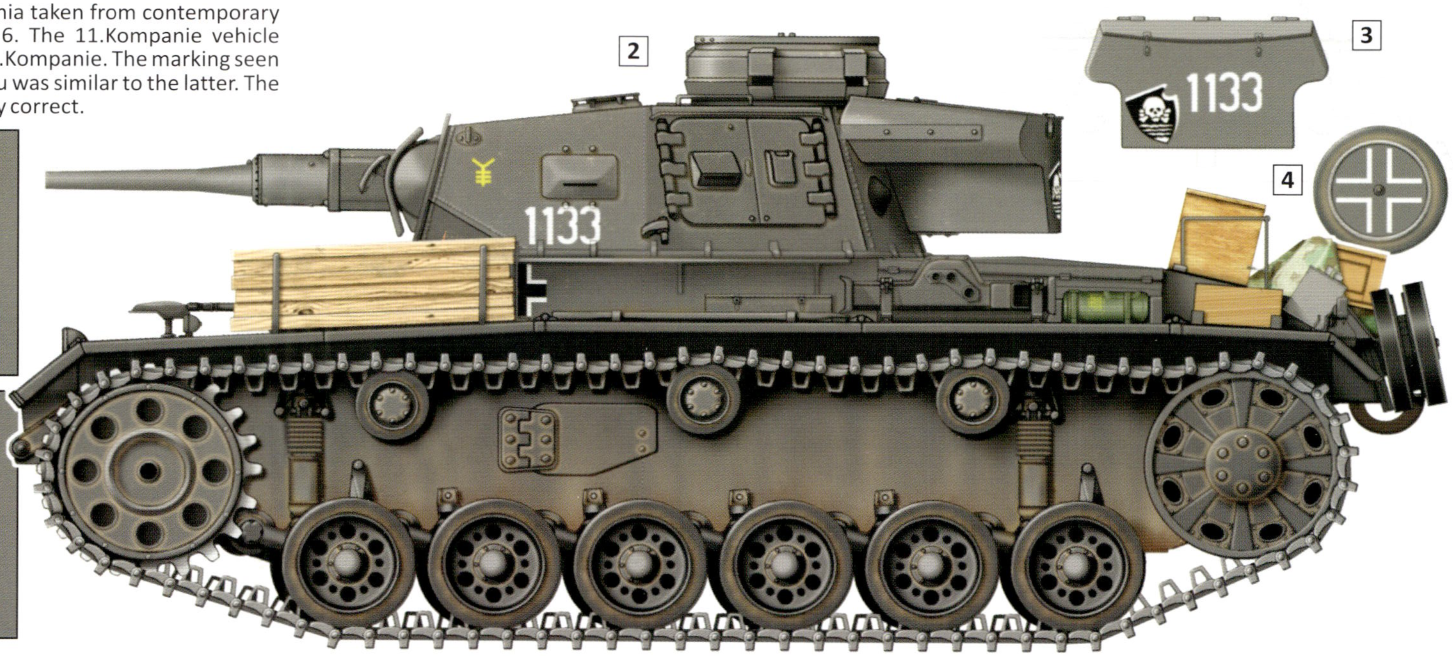

Below: Examples of the Panzer-Regiment 18 unit insignia taken from contemporary photographs. 5. The I.Abteilung tank shown above. 6. The 11.Kompanie vehicle depicted at right. 7. and 8. A Pzkpfw IV Tauchpanzer of 9.Kompanie. The marking seen on the III.Abteilung Befehlspanzer of Major von Zeschau was similar to the latter. The use of yellow as a border is assumed but almost certainly correct.

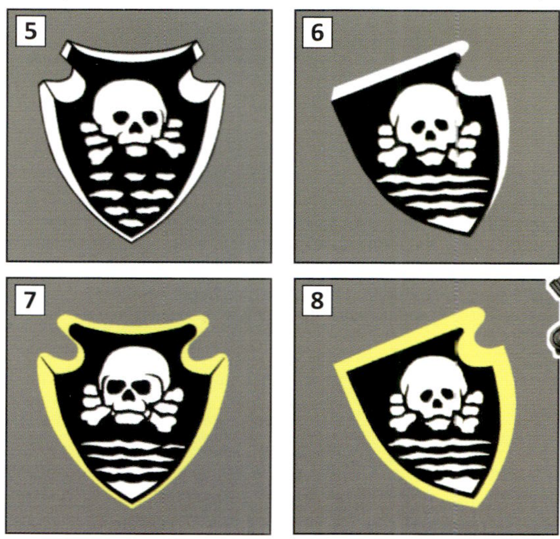

1. Panzerbefehlswagen III ausf H. Panzer-Brigade 18. Ukraine, summer 1941. Assigned to Panzergruppe Guderian for the invasion of the Soviet Union, 18.Panzer-Division was one of the few formations to retain an armoured brigade headquarters. The brigade probably contained two of these purpose-built command tanks.

2. Pzkpfw III ausf H. 3.Kompanie, Panzer-Abteilung zbV 40. Finland, summer 1941. Most of this company's tanks seem to have lacked the Rommelkiste or stowage box which was common by this time. The company number was repeated on the turret rear (3) and another, very clear, image of this tank shows that the turret roof and cupola hatch were painted white (4). Note that the MG 34, mounted in the hull front, is fitted with an armoured sleeve

1

3

2

4

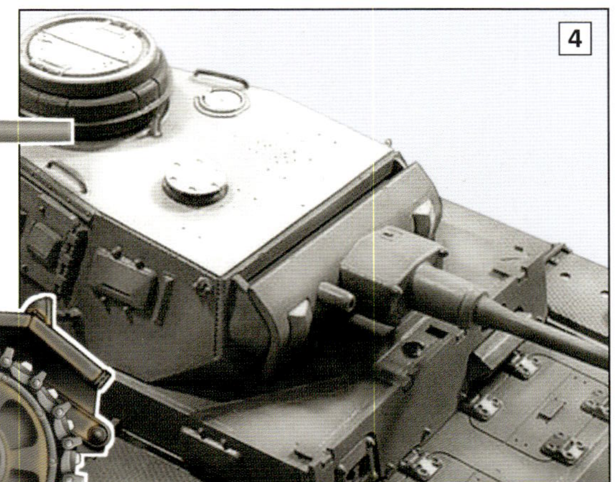

2

1

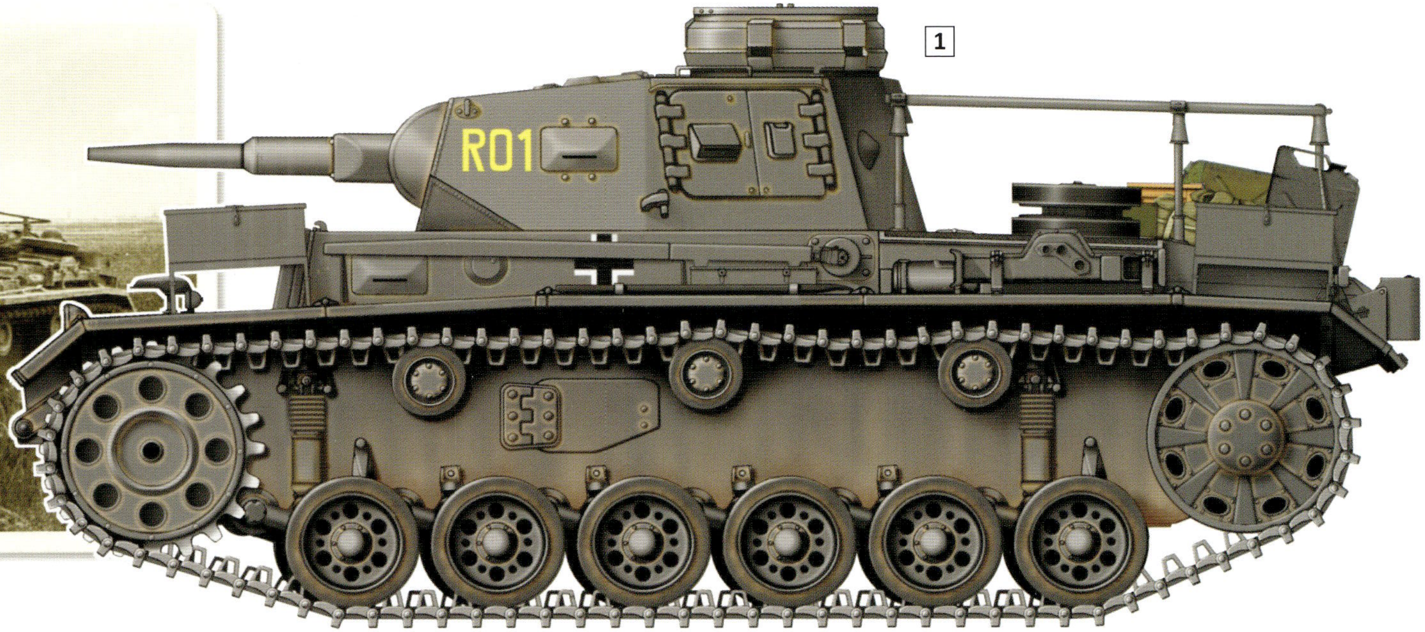

4

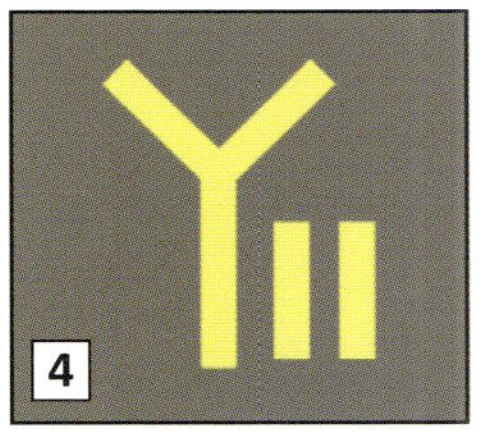

3

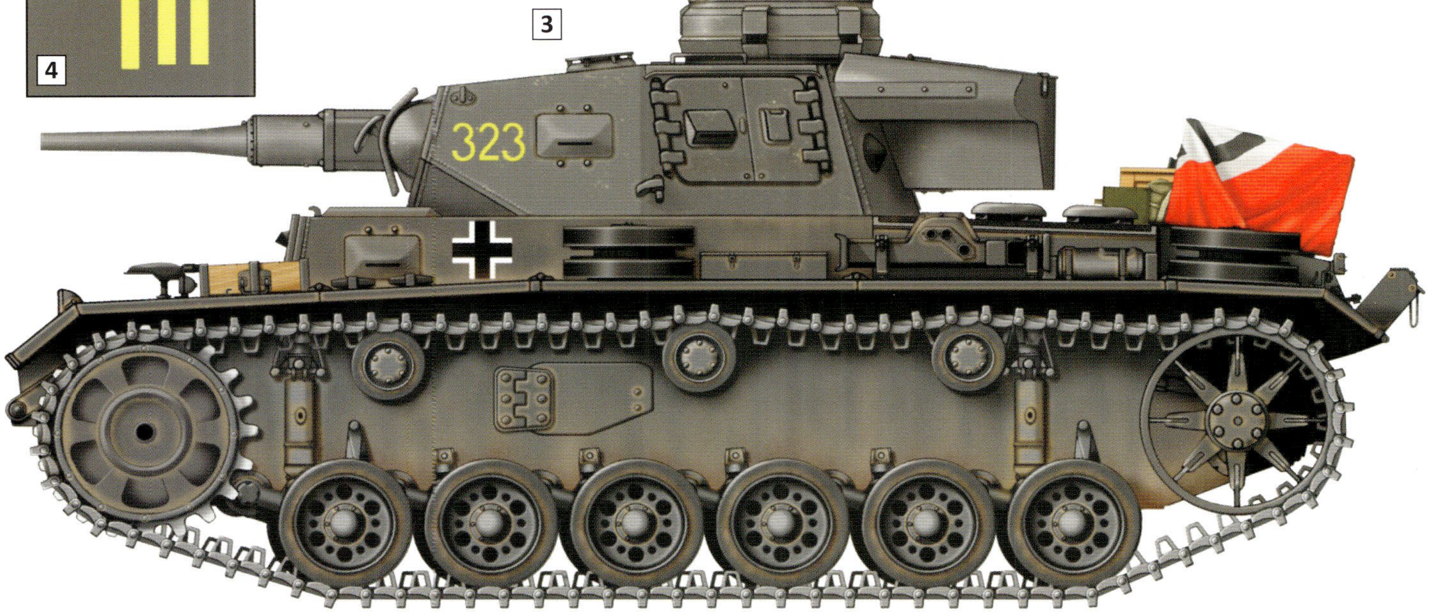

1. Panzerbefehlswagen III ausf H. Stab, Panzer-Regiment 33. Southern Ukraine, summer 1941. The large stowage boxes, fitted on both sides and the front and rear, were an identifying feature of this regiment's command tanks and are clearly visible in our photograph (2). This tank seems to have no markings other than the turret number which identifies the regimental commander.

3. Pzkpfw III ausf G. 3.Kompanie, Panzer-Regiment 33. Ukraine, summer 1941. This vehicle is one of the earlier models upgraded from August 1940 as part of the so-called Umbewaffnung programme and fitted with the 5cm gun, widened suspension and Tropen ventilation system. These upgrades are discussed further in the Technical Details & Modifications section of this book. This regiment used the standard numbering system where the company, platoon and individual tank could be identified and the numbers were almost certainly rendered in yellow. The division's official unit insignia (4) was painted onto the hull front between the driver's visor and the machine-gun mount.

1

1. Pzkpfw III ausf J. 1.Kompanie, Panzer-Regiment 35. Russia, summer 1941. This model of the Pzkpfw III was the most numerous in terms of production but as the first examples left the assembly lines in March 1941 they were still a comparatively rare sight during the summer battles in the East. The regiment's unit insignia of a standing bear was rendered in solid white for 1.Kompanie, as were the turret numbers. I can offer no explanation as to the significance of the black and white geometric logo painted onto the hull side but it is quite clear in the well-known series of photographs of this tank.

2

2. Pzkpfw III ausf H Tauchpanzer. 2.Kompanie, Panzer-Regiment 35. Russia, summer 1941. The regiment's unit insignia was applied with what is almost certainly a red centre for 2.Kompanie tanks and from this we can probably assume that 3.Kompanie, and perhaps the Stabs-Kompanie, also used different colours. Note the official unit insignia on the hull side and also at the front which is clearly visible in our photograph (3).

3

1

2

1. Pzkpfw III ausf H Tauchpanzer. 5.Kompanie, Panzer-Regiment 36. Russia, summer 1941. Of note are the unusual extensions fitted to the special exhausts clearly visible in our photograph (2). Other aspects of these submersible tanks are discussed in the Technical Details & Modifications section of this book. The photograph also illustrates how dark RAL Schwartzgrau actually was, appearing almost black in many contemporary colour images. The unit insignia of 14.Panzer-Division, to which this regiment was attached, is painted onto the turret side above the company number.

3

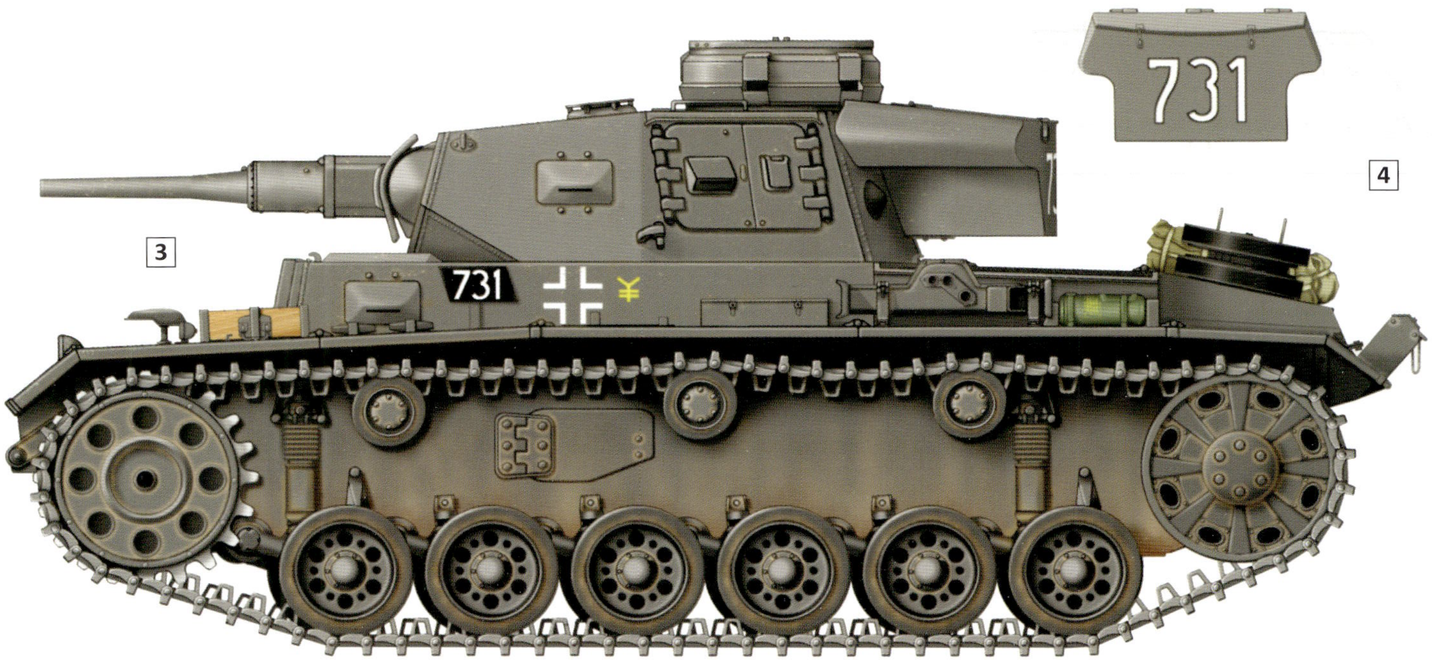

4

3. Pzkpfw III ausf G. 7.Kompanie, Panzer-Regiment 39. Russia, summer 1941. The method of displaying the tank's company number by means of the detachable small metal rhomboid fixed to the hull side was common during the early Blitzkrieg campaigns but is less frequently encountered in 1941. Note that the number on the rear of the stowage box (4) is rendered in a completely different style. The official unit insignia of 17.Panzer-Division is painted onto the hull side in yellow and was probably repeated at the front.

3

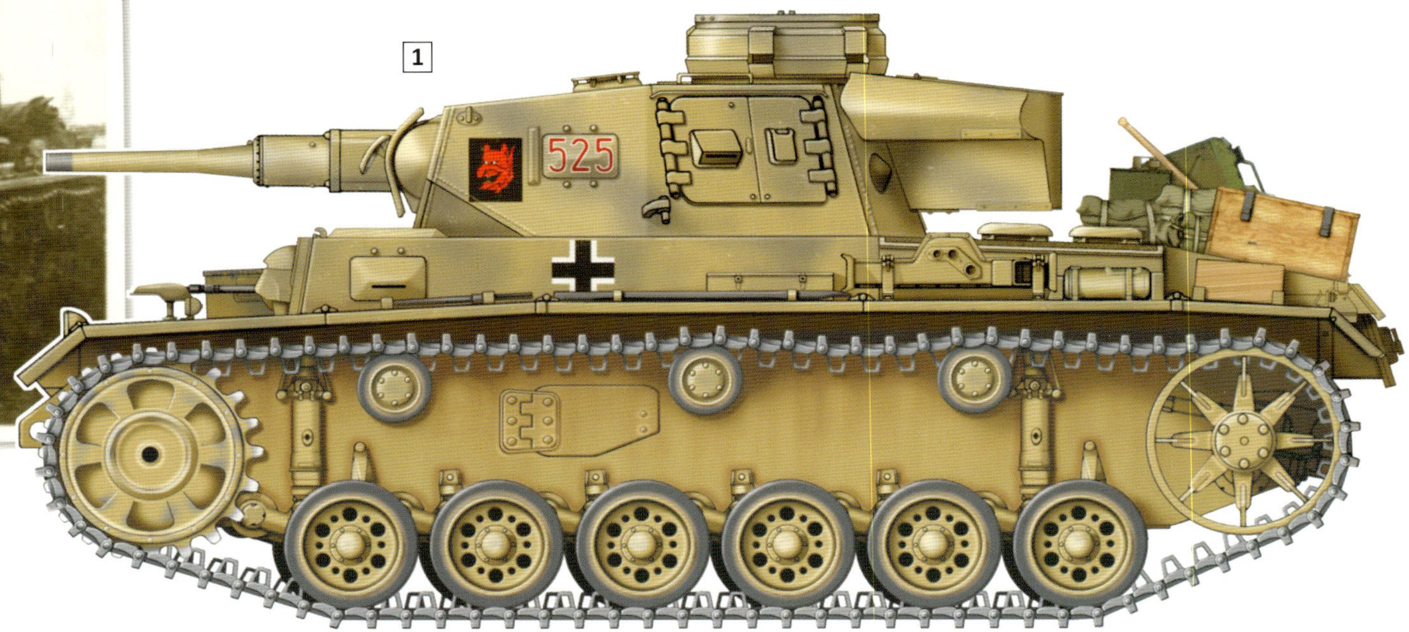

1

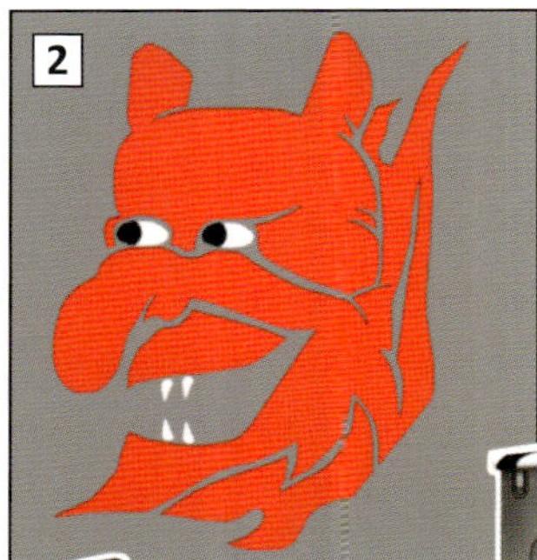

2

4

1. Pzkpfw III ausf J. 5.Kompanie, Panzer-Regiment 31. Germany, autumn 1941. This regiment, attached to 5.Panzer-Division, took part in the Balkan campaign and was refitting in Germany when Operation Barbarossa commenced. Originally earmarked for service in North Africa, the division was eventually sent to the Eastern Front in September 1941 and it has been suggested that the tropical camouflage in which the tanks were painted was not changed before the move to Russia. The contrast between the division's unit insignia (2)and the tank's base coat evident in our photograph (3) would indicate that this is indeed true here. However, the regiment's 5.Kompanie was detached and transferred to Crete in July 1941 and this could be one of those tanks. The colour scheme rendered here is a base of RAL 8000 Gelbbraun with a light disruptive pattern in RAL 7008 Grau which was introduced in March 1941 for units serving in the Mediterranean.

4. Pzkpfw III ausf J. 1.Kompanie, Panzer-Regiment 31. Russia, winter 1941. With the onset of winter and the first real coverage of snow, German vehicles were camouflaged with whatever white material came to hand. Whitewash was officially sanctioned but chalk and even bed sheets can be seen in contemporary photographs. Although the whitewash camouflage depicted here has been applied sparingly, and quite roughly, the division's unit insignia and the tank's company number have been carefully avoided.

PZKPFW III AUSF G

PANZER-REGIMENT 3

1/35 SCALE

MIKE TIPPING

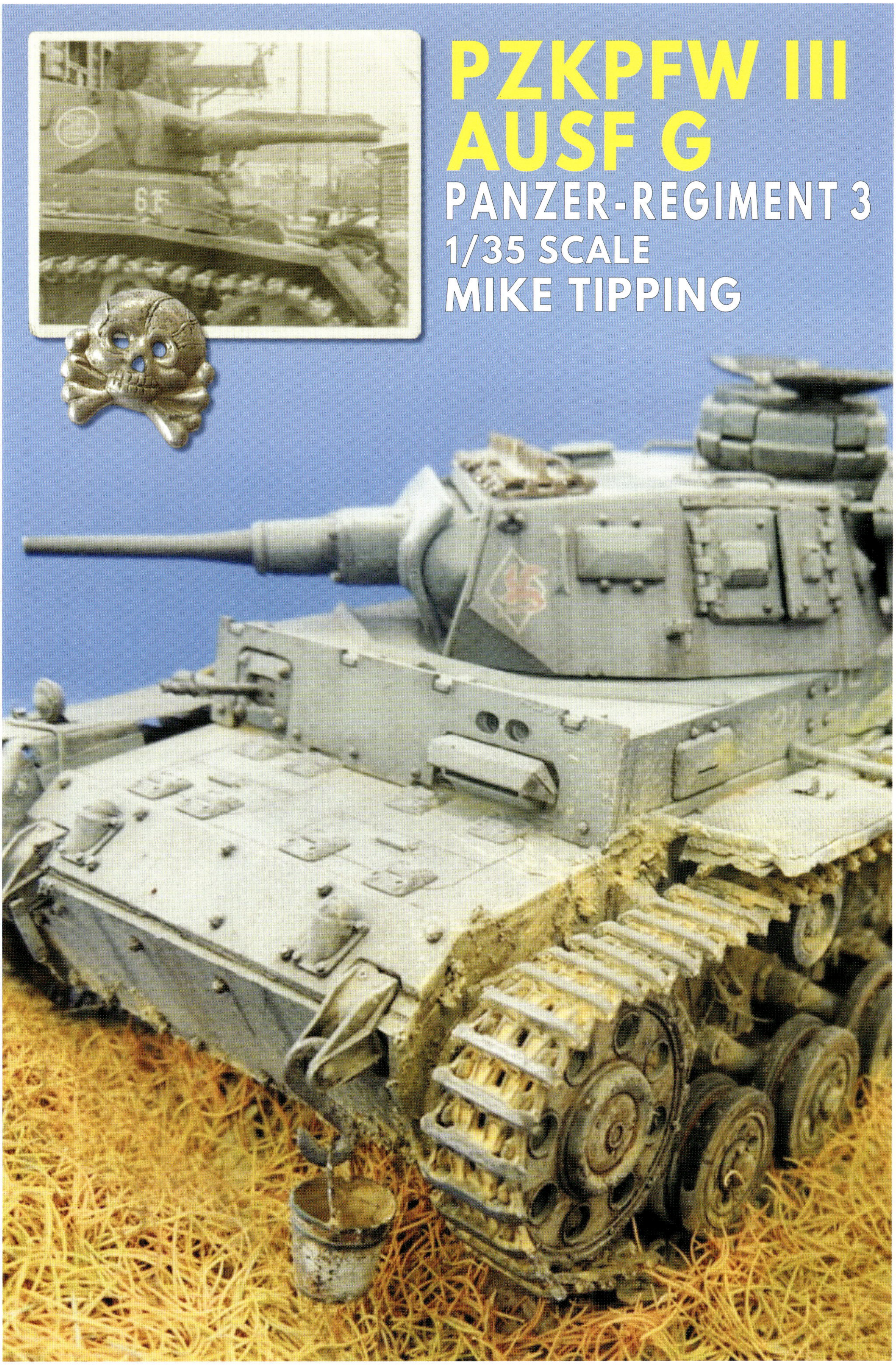

British modeller Mike Tipping's replica is based on Tamiya's 1/35 scale kit with many scratch-built and modified parts. The model has also been back dated with the addition of the early drive sprocket, rear idler and shock absorbers.

A rear view of Mike's Pzkpfw III ausf G. Note the metal bracket holding the stowage bin, colloquially referred to as the Rommelkiste, to the turret. This was a feature of the early upgraded versions of this tank.

A front view showing the bolted-on additional armour of the hull front and glacis and the early style towing eyes. It will probably come as no surprise that Mike is a professional modeller and accepts commissions for armour and aircraft models. His contact details are given on page 64.

PZKPFW III AUSF J

PANZER-REGIMENT 36

1/35 SCALE

MASAHIRO DOI

Japanese modeller Masahiro Doi used the Tamiya 1/35 scale Pzkpfw III ausf L kit to create this model of an early production Pzkpfw III ausf J. Some details, including the unditching beam on the hull side, were scratch-built, while the rest was made using parts from the kit. The finished project was painted with Creos Mr Color Lacquer paints, including the markings, and the crew figures were sculpted by Masahiro.

PZKPFW III AUSF J

PANZER-REGIMENT 2

1/48 SCALE

MASAHIRO DOI

Masahiro used the Tamyia 1/48 scale Pzkpfw III ausf L model and incorporated a number of earlier production features such as the 3.7cm gun, the hull side escape hatches and the turret vision ports to create this earlier variant. The model was painted and weathered entirely with artist's gouache.

The rear deck, and lack of Tropen air intake covers, was another feature of these early production tanks. The markings used by Panzer-Regiment 2 of 16.Panzer-Division are explained on page 26 of the Camouflage & Markings section of this book.

PZKPFW III AUSF H
TAUCHPANZER
PANZER-REGIMENT 2
1/35 SCALE
SUNGJUN JANG

Korean modeller Sungjun Jang based his replica on the 1/35 scale Dragon Models Tauchpanzer III ausf H which was first released in 2015. The model also incorporates photo-etched brass parts from Voyager Model which readers of this series will be familiar with.

By 1941 the complicated breathing apparatus of these submersible tanks had largely been replaced by a simple snorkel, here carried on the hull side with the unditching beam. When required, the snorkel was attached to the turret roof through the periscope hatch next to the commander's cupola.

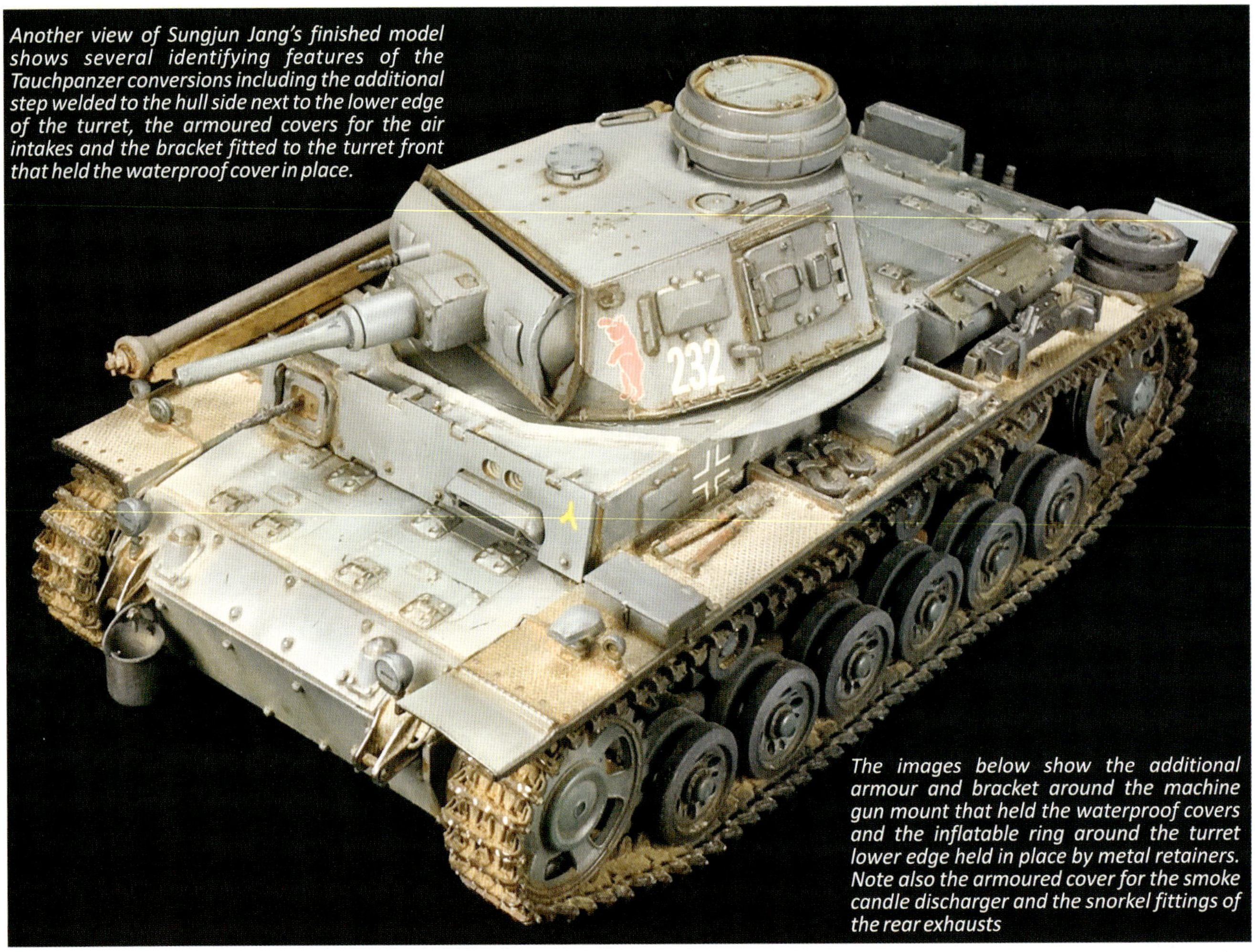

Another view of Sungjun Jang's finished model shows several identifying features of the Tauchpanzer conversions including the additional step welded to the hull side next to the lower edge of the turret, the armoured covers for the air intakes and the bracket fitted to the turret front that held the waterproof cover in place.

The images below show the additional armour and bracket around the machine gun mount that held the waterproof covers and the inflatable ring around the turret lower edge held in place by metal retainers. Note also the armoured cover for the smoke candle discharger and the snorkel fittings of the rear exhausts

PZKPFW III
AUSF F & AUSF A
1/35 SCALE
SUNGJUN JANG

Although the models shown here depict vehicles that served in the French and Polish campaigns I have included them as many Pzkpfw III ausf F tanks were still in service in 1941 and they illustrate the distinctive suspension of the Pzkpfw III ausf A. The latter is based on the Bronco Models kit while the Pzkpfw III ausf F is from Dragon Models. Both are in 1/35 scale.

The Pzkpfw III, and its contemporary the Pzkpfw IV, were arguably the most important armoured vehicles of the Blitzkrieg period. The first plastic kits of this light tank were probably those released by Tamiya in 1/21 scale in the early 1960s and even by the standards of the day these were very inaccurate representations. The 1/30 scale Pzkpfw III ausf E model offered by Nichimo a few years later, while lacking fine detail, was largely correct in shape and outline. With the decision to concentrate on a constant scale of 1/35 in 1970, Tamiya produced a totally new kit marketed as Panzerkampfwagen III Ausf. M/N and this was a major step forward in detail and accuracy. At about the same time, companies such as Otaki, Hasegawa and Fujimi in Japan, ESCI in Italy and Matchbox in Britain began releasing kits of the Pzkpfw III in both 1/35, 1/72 and 1/76 scale and although these were quite good models, most represented the later versions armed with the long-barrelled 5cm gun, additional armour and Schürzen for the turret and hull. Many of these old kits have been re-boxed and released under the logos of several companies in the intervening years.

From 1987 Gunze Sangyo released a series of highly detailed models and these kits, although somewhat expensive, introduced a large audience to the concept of a multi-media kit, containing plastic sprues with photo-etched brass and white metal details and optional barrels in turned aluminium. The company's first offering was a 1/35 scale Pzkpfw III ausf J and this model formed the basis for the extensive range of kits later released by Dragon Models. The last few decades have seen something of a boom in the plastic model industry and kits of the Pzkpfw III are currently available in sizes ranging from 1/285 scale wargames tanks to massive 1/6 scale radio-controlled vehicles.

As with the other books in this series, I have chosen to concentrate on the most popular modelling scales of 1/35 and 1/48, although I have tried to include some of the smaller scale models and also the very early versions of this important tank which are now easily accessible for the first time.

As many manufacturers regularly withdraw products from their catalogues, often only to be repackaged and re-released at some later date, I have tried to include models which are readily available at the time of writing and where this is not so I have tried to make it clear. Similarly, as this title deals with the tanks that took part in Operation Barbarossa I have endeavoured, for the most part, to include versions of the Pzkpfw III which would have been the most commonly encountered during the battles of the late summer and the autumn of 1941. An index of manufacturers, with their contact details, can be found on page 64.

TAMIYA INC

This Japanese company, the largest model manufacturer in the world, has produced an extensive range of armoured vehicles, with complementary figures and accessories, and was almost solely responsible for the rise in popularity of 1/35 scale. Although rather basic by today's standards, the kits released from the early 1970s were highly accurate and detailed when compared to what else was available at the time. Importantly, they were easy to build and affordable and, like Airfix before them, Tamiya kits were all made to a common scale which encouraged modellers to build a collection. The company's monopoly of the 1/35 scale market remained unchallenged until the release of the first Dragon Models kits in 1987. In 2003 Tamiya began releasing models in 1/48 scale and this has been extremely successful for the company, combining the potential for detail without the expense of the bigger kits. The current catalogue lists a Pzkpfw III ausf L and ausf N in both 1/35 and 1/48 scale and although both versions were introduced into service after 1941 I have included them here as they served as a basis for a number of the kits shown in the Model Showcase section of this book. I should mention that they cannot be built as the earlier versions without extra parts.

Masahiro Doi's early production Pzkpfw III ausf J model based on Tamiya's 1/48 scale Pzkpfw III ausf L, shown in the background. Although the Tamiya kit does include some early features as optional extras, such as the hull side escape hatches, it does not come with the short 3.7cm gun or appropriate markings.

DRAGON MODELS LTD

Dragon Models was one of the first of the major manufacturers to offer accurate replicas in 1/35 scale and their kits are today something of a benchmark. The company's small scale releases are some of the best available. At the time of writing this Hong Kong-based company offered in 1/35 scale a Pzkpfw III ausf E/F, an ausf G, as a Tauchpanzer and with the Tropen air intakes, an ausf H in early and late production versions and also as a Befehlspanzerwagen, and an ausf J in both 1/35 and 1/72 scale which can be built as a number of variants. All these kits have been re-boxed at some time, usually with different markings, and some include photo-etched brass parts.

Above: A selection of Dragon Models' Pzkpfw III kits in 1/35 and 1/72 scale. Although they are marketed as being specific to a period or campaign, these models can all be built as tanks that took part in Operation Barbarossa.

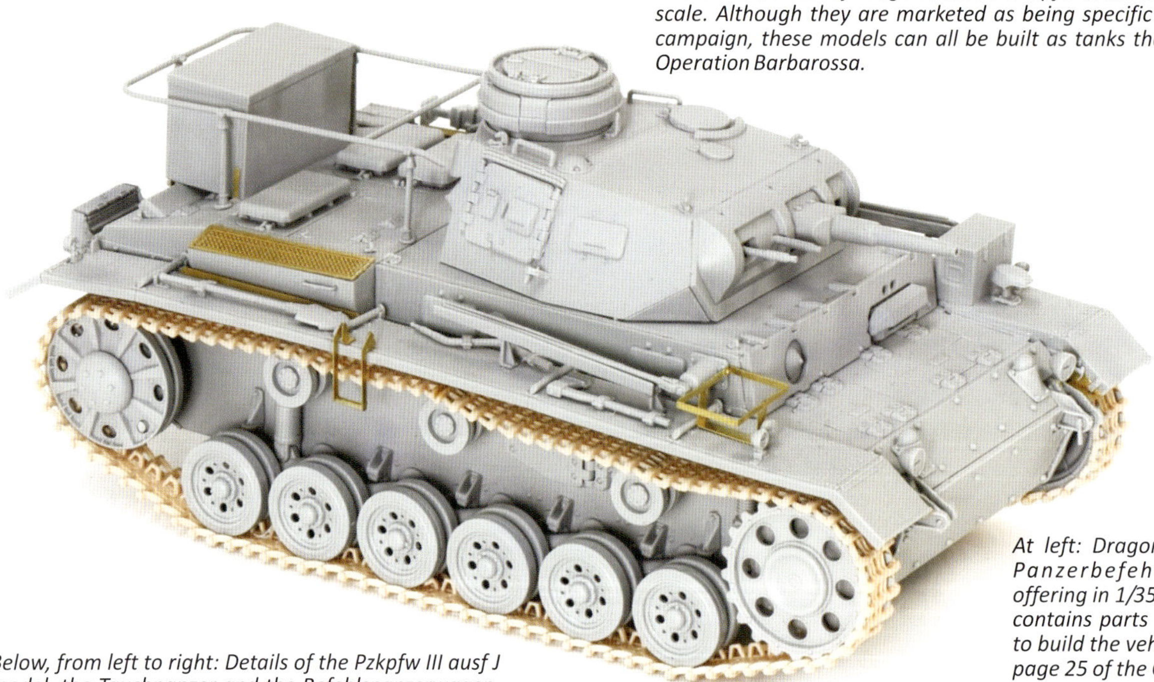

At left: Dragon's 1/35 scale Panzerbefehlswagen III offering in 1/35 scale. This kit contains parts and markings to build the vehicle shown on page 25 of the Camouflage & Markings section.

Below, from left to right: Details of the Pzkpfw III ausf J model, the Tauchpanzer and the Befehlspanzerwagen, both based on the Pzkpfw III ausf H, all in 1/35 scale.

BRACH MODEL

Since 1996 this Italian company has been offering an extensive range of highly detailed and accurate model replicas of tanks, aircraft and figures in addition to upgrade sets. Although the complete kits can be rather expensive they do represent unusual or rare vehicles such as the Durchbruchswagen 2, from which the Tiger was eventually developed, and the Kleinetraktor I. Thay also contain many optional parts. Shown below is the 1/35 scale kit of the Pzkpfw III ausf B which contains resin and photo-etched elements as well as a turned aluminium barrel. This version of the Pzkpfw III had been relegated to training roles by the time of Operation Barbarossa.

MINIART

Based in Ukraine, this company has been producing high quality plastic models since 2001. Their catalogue contains a large number of building and diorama accessories and crew figures in 1/35 scale. Starting in 2014, Miniart released a series based on the very early versions of the Pzkpfw III and although very few of these served in Russia, as explained in the main text, they deserve at least some mention here. Shown below is the Pzkpfw III ausf D and the box art of the ausf B model.

Although most of these early development versions of the Pzkpfw III were operating with training units by 1941, at least four, confirmed by photographic evidence, served with Panzer-Abteilung zbV 40 in northern Russia in 1941.

ATTACK HOBBY KITS

This Czech company has been producing scale model tanks since 1992, mostly in the smaller scales. Some of the earlier kits, such as the Panzerbefehlswagen III, lack detail but the most recent offerings are of a higher quality and very easy to build. Shown below are details of the Pzkpfw III ausf J in 1/72 scale. The Ostketten tracks are optional and are of course not appropriate for the period covered by this book. The basic hull shown at left is finished with photo-etched detail from Hauler.

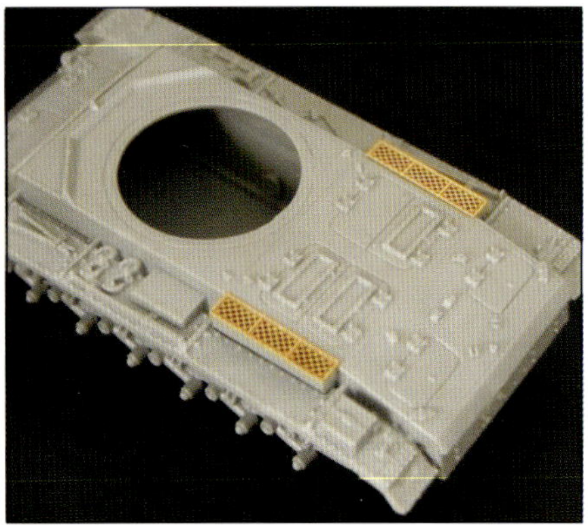

FIRST TO FIGHT

This is a recently-formed company that specialises in producing 1/72 scale versions of the vehicles used by the main protagonists of the 1939 Polish campaign. In addition to tanks there are a number of armoured car and figure sets. Shown below is the company's Pzkpfw III ausf E, offered in both the standard production and command tank versions. These models are reasonably detailed but essentially aimed at the wargamer, evidenced by the simplified construction shown at right.

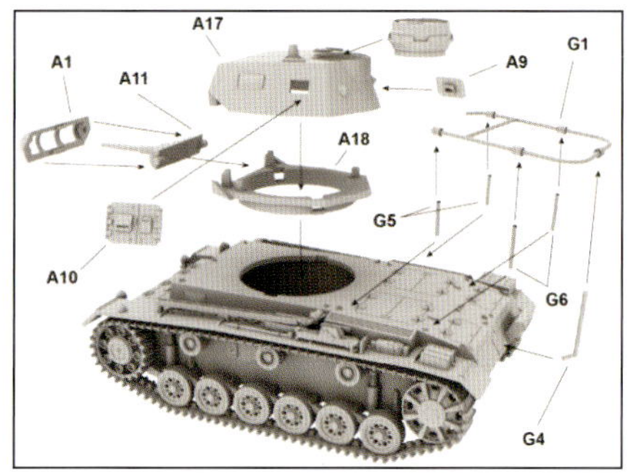

MILICAST MODELS

Based in Glasgow, this company was founded in 1985 and has continually upgraded and refined its huge range of 1/76 scale tanks, armoured cars and other vehicles since that time. In 2004 Milicast introduced a range specificly aimed at wargamers, referred to as the Battlefield Range, while the more detailed models were marketed as the Premier Range. Shown below are, 1. Pzkpfw III ausf F. This is the early production version. 2. An upgraded Pzkpfw III ausf G. 3. A Pzkfpfw III ausf H. All models are from the Battlefield Range and would be suitable for the time period covered by this book.

VOYAGER MODEL

Voyager Model, based in Shanghai, have been manufacturing upgrade sets for scale models since 2003 with the release of their first set for 1/35 scale armour. The company produces a number of items in both 1/72 and 1/35 scale in photo-etched brass and also resin, including wheel hubs, damaged road wheels, ammunition crates and boxes and fuel containers. Voyager also offers highly detailed and accurate gun barrels in milled aluminium and brass. Shown below are details from Voyager's upgrade sets for, 1 to 3. Pzkpfw III ausf E/F. 4 to 6. Pzkpfw III ausf E through to the early ausf H.

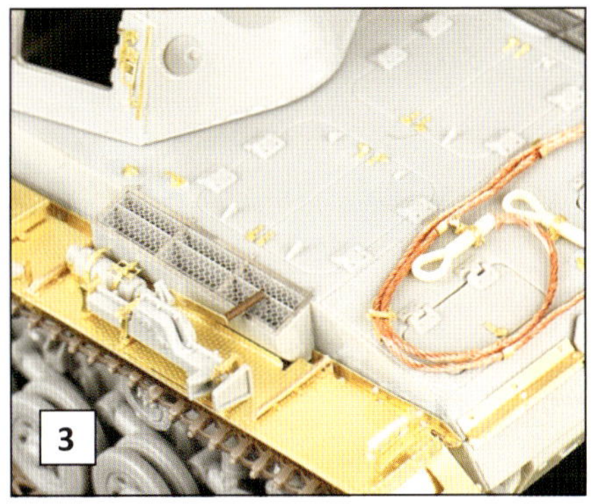

ABER

This Polish company has been manufacturing and selling upgrade sets since 1995, working in photo-etched brass, milled aluminium, stainless steel and even wood. For some time now Tamiya has included a number of Aber products with their models. A full list of the accessories made specifically for the Pzkpfw III in all scales would be far too long to list on this page, particularly in light of the company's regular new releases, and the reader can find the company's contact details on page 64. Shown below are. 1. Detail of the upgrade set for the 1/35 scale Dragon kit. 2. A turned aluminium barrel of the 3.7cm gun in 1/35 scale. 3. A 1/35 scale Pzkpfw III stowage bin in photo-etched brass. 4, 5 and 6. Details of Aber's upgrade set for the Tamiya 1/48 scale model.

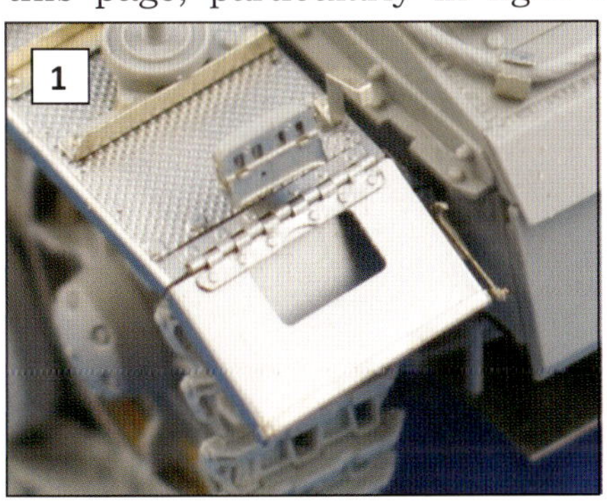

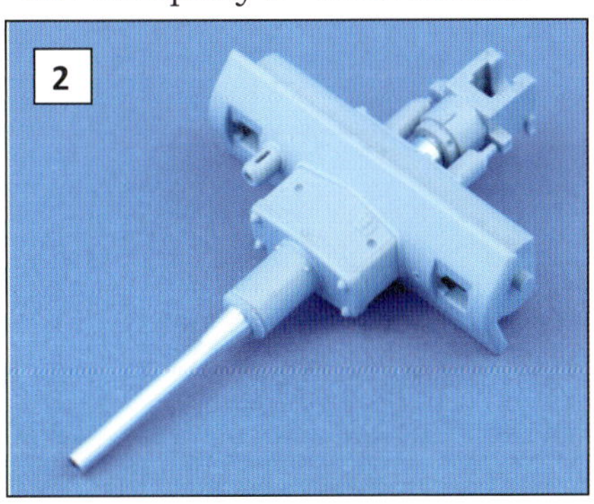

RB MODEL

RB Model from Poland produce a range of milled aluminium and brass gun barrels and resin accessories for 1/72, 1/48 and 1/35 scale armour models. Shown below, from left to right, are the beautifully detailed 3.7cm and 5cm gun barrels in 1/35 scale and a tiny barrel for an MG 34 in 1/48 scale. RB Model also offers a large selection of generic accessories such as radio antenna insulators, towing shackles, ammunition crates and fuel containers.

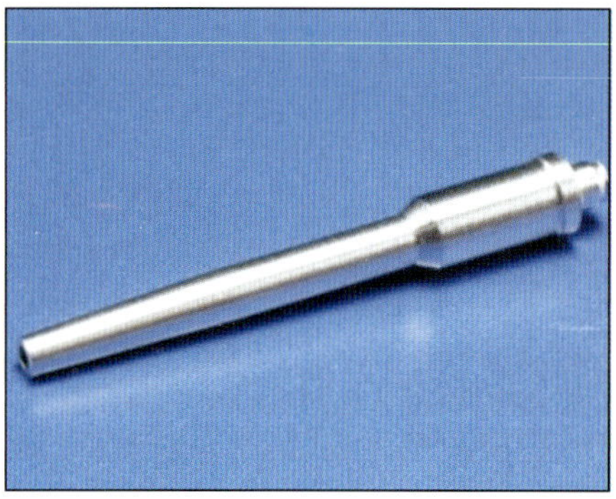

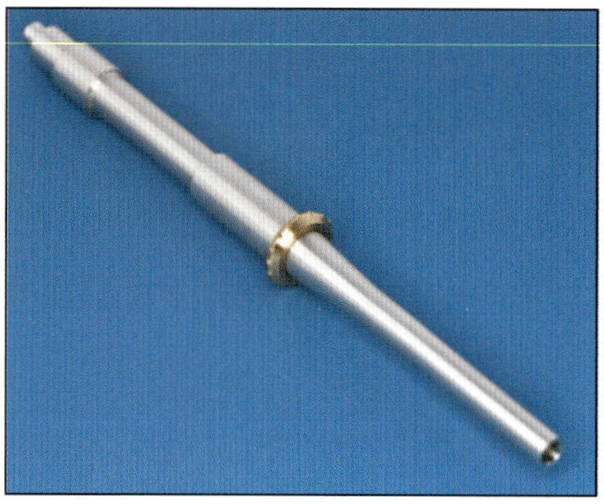

EDUARD MODEL ACCESSORIES

Founded in 1989, this Czech company produces high quality upgrade kits in photo-etched metal and resin and a number of scale models. Currently available are extensive photo-etched detail sets to update the Pzkpfw III models marketed by Tamiya, Dragon Models, including the ausf J versions, and the Pzkpfw III ausf F from Zvezda. The latter, a re-boxed version of the Gunze Sangyo kit, seems to have been dropped from the company's catalogue but is offered for sale by many retailers.

Below, and at the bottom of the page: The Zvezda 1/35 scale Pzkpfw III ausf F build with Eduard Model Accessories' photo-etched brass upgrade set. Most of these parts would be suitable for other versions of this tank.

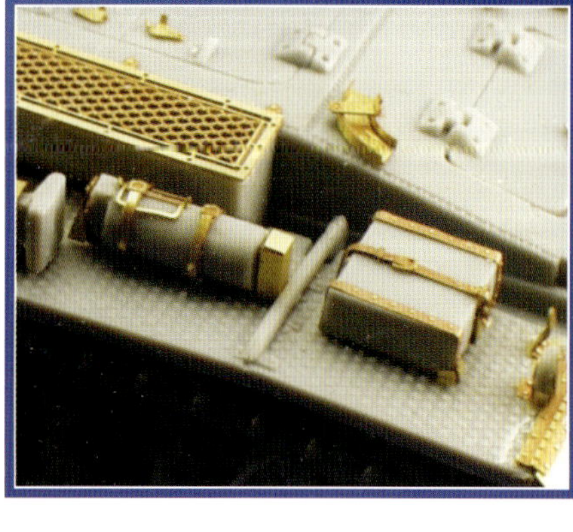

E.T. MODEL

This company, based in China, produces upgrade sets in 1/72 and 1/35 scale in brass and resin. Although most sets are specifically designed, according to the company, to fit Dragon or Tamiya kits, some parts or accessories, for example the stowage bins, are referred to as universal.

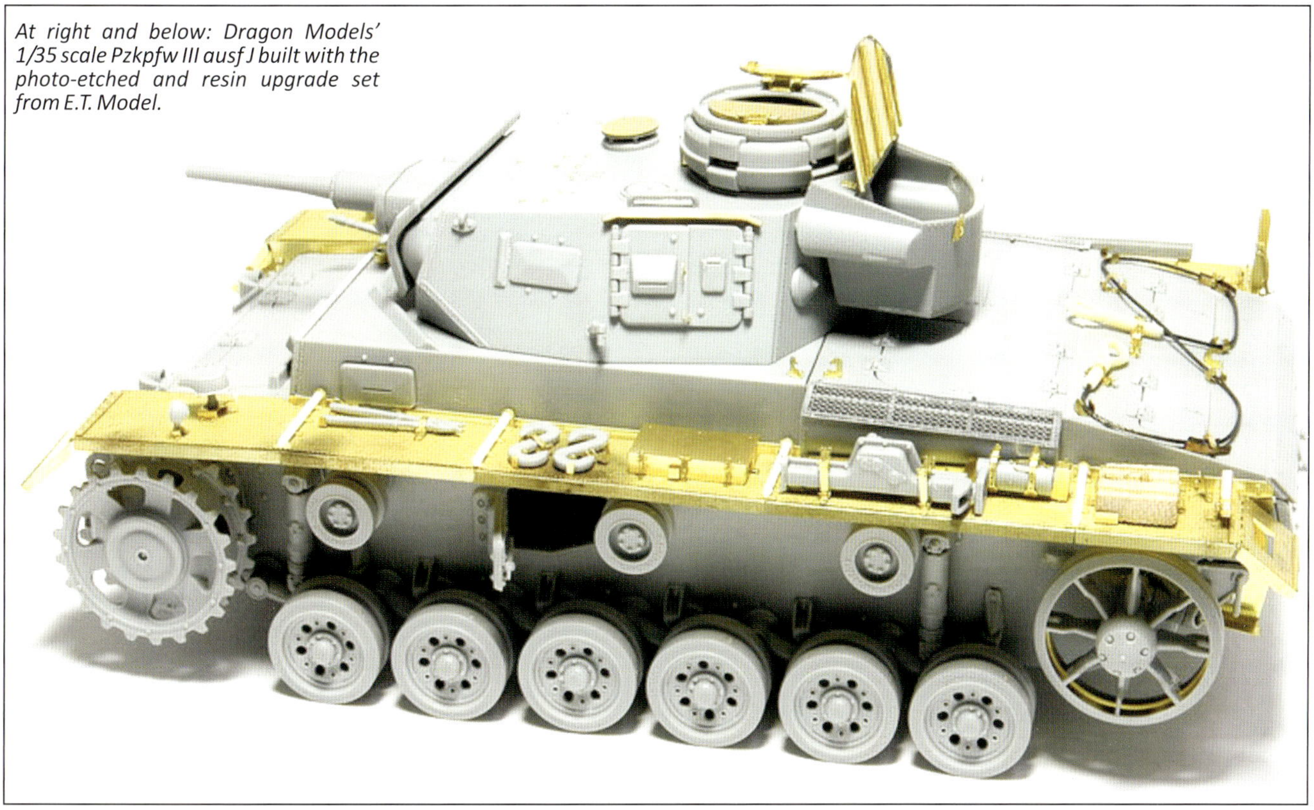

At right and below: Dragon Models' 1/35 scale Pzkpfw III ausf J built with the photo-etched and resin upgrade set from E.T. Model.

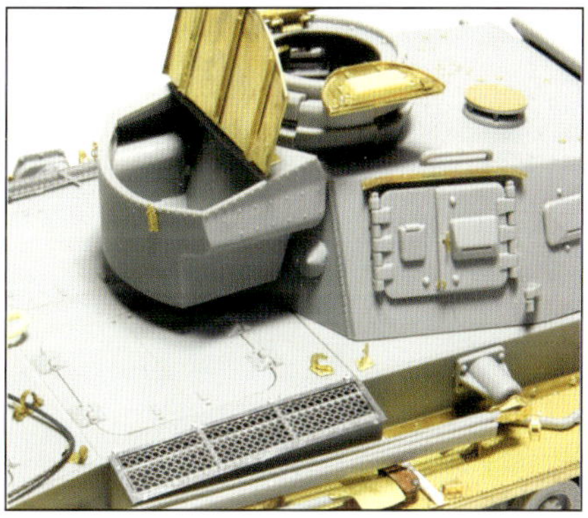

PANZER ART

Based in Poland, this company produces a large range of resin parts for Second World War and modern era armoured vehicles in 1/35 scale. Shown here, are: 1. Canvas cover, mantlet and brass MG 34 barrel for the 3.7cm gun. 2. Canvas cover and gun mantlet for the 5cm gun. 3. Later-style drive sprocket which was introduced towards the end of the Pzkpfw III ausf G production run.

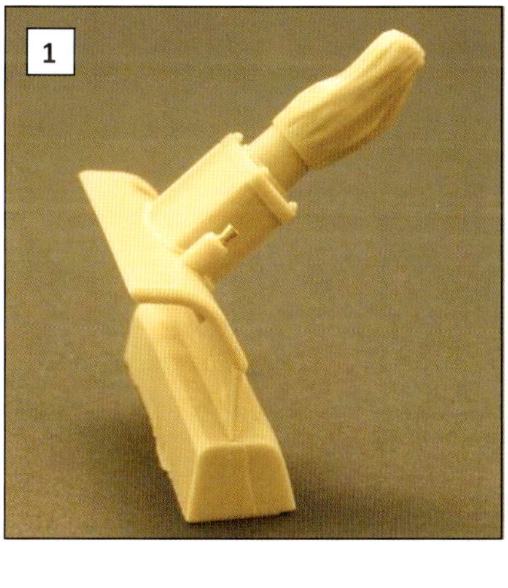

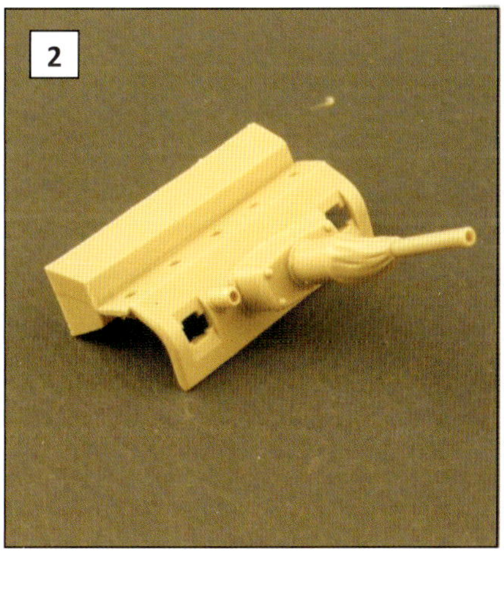

BLACK DOG

Based in the Czech Republic, this company produces a large range of detailed resin accessory and upgrade sets for armoured vehicles in 1/35, 1/48 and 1/72 scale and a small number of complete kits. Although the accessories shown here are marketed as appropriate to later models of the Pzkpfw III, most would be suitable for the 1941 Russian Front campaign.

AFTERMARKET TRACKS

Most plastic kits today contain realistic tracks made from either a form of vinyl which, unlike the older types, can be glued together or hard plastic individual links. Nevertheless, there are many modellers who wish for the highest level of detail and realism possible and consequently the number of quality aftermarket products available seems to have increased in recent years, despite the extra expense and work required. In order to operate properly, motorised models require workable tracks made up from individual links held together by pins, as were the full-size items.

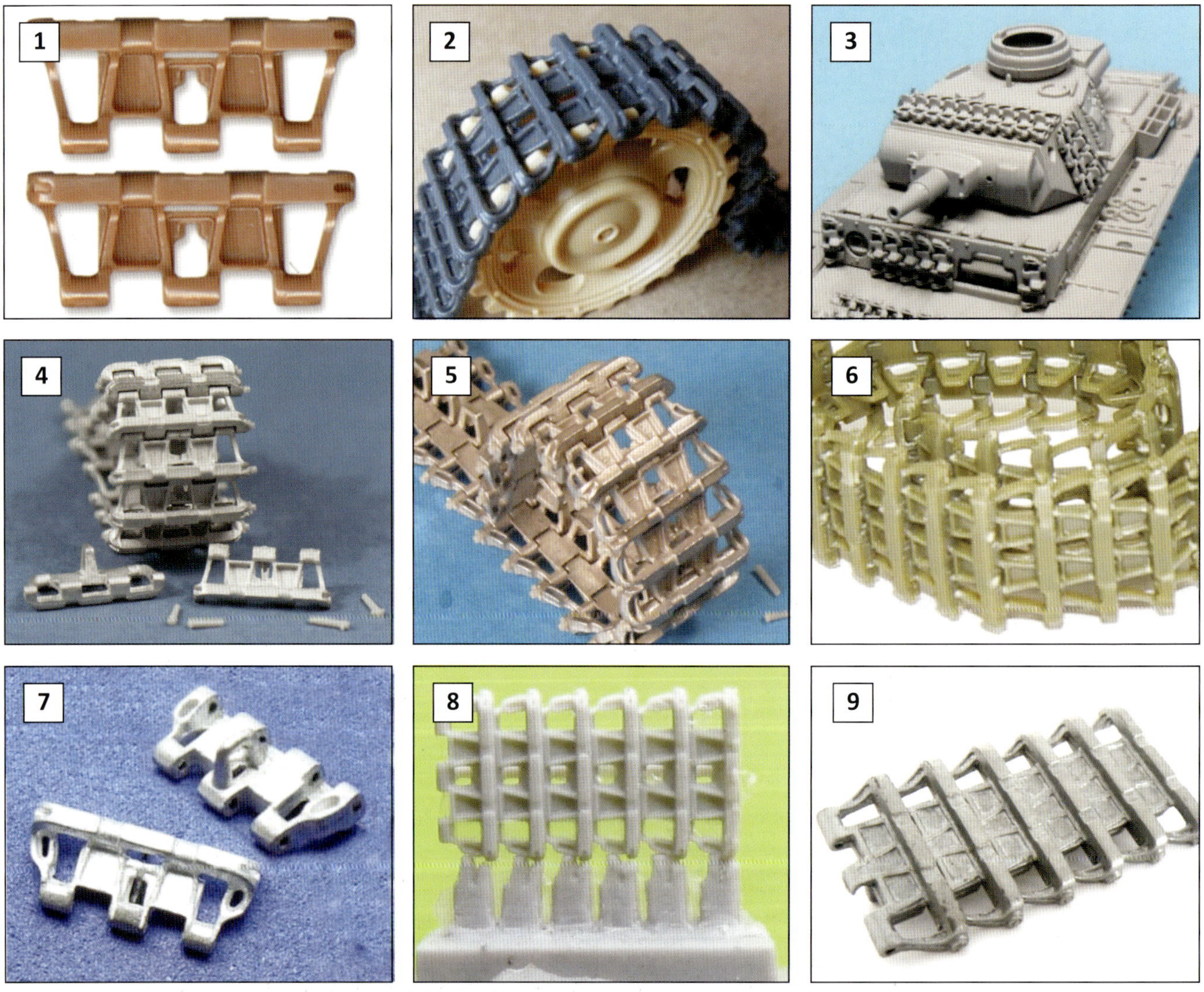

Above: A selection of aftermarket tracks. 1. Individual Modelkasten Pzkpfw III tracks in 1/35 scale. 2. Kaizen early pattern tracks in 1/35 scale. 3. 1/72 scale spare tracks from JK Resin. These are not workable links. 4. 1/35 scale early Pzkpfw III tracks. 5. Pzkpfw III tracks introduced in 1941 from Masterclub in 1/35 scale. 6. Fully workable plastic tracks from Miniart. These tracks, and the Pzkpfw III kits, come with a jig to help with assembly. 7. 1/35 scale from Spade Ace Models. 8. 1/72 scale from OB Grigorov. 9. 1/16 scale from OzArmour specifically designed fro the Hen Long model. This is in fact a length of spare track but the company does offer fully assembled workable tracks.

...........continued from page 16

5.Panzer-Division. Formed in November 1938, the division fought in Poland, France and the Balkans before being transferred to Germany to be rebuilt.

Many accounts state that the division took part in the fighting on Crete in May 1941 but just two Pzkpfw II tanks were involved and these were ferried to the island on the initiative of a junior Kriegsmarine officer. Parts of the Panzer regiment's 5.Kompanie were later used to build Panzer-Abteilung 212, also known as Panzer-Abteilung Kreta, which was stationed on the island.

In July 1941 the division was ordered to prepare for service in North Africa but the order was eventually rescinded and on Thursday, 11 September 1941 the first units of 5.Panzer-Division began arriving on the Eastern Front. At that time the division's Panzer-Regiment 31 was outfitted with fifty-five Pzkpfw II, twenty Pzkpfw IV and 105 Pzkpfw III tanks. Most, if not all, of the latter would have been armed with the 5cm gun.

From 2 October 1941, as part of Panzergruppe 4, the division took part in Operation Typhoon, the attack on Moscow, and the battles around Vyazma. Units of 5.Panzer-Division were advancing towards the Istra River crossing on the road to Krasnogorsk, today a north-western suburb of Moscow, when the Russian counteroffensive began in early December, forcing the Germans back.

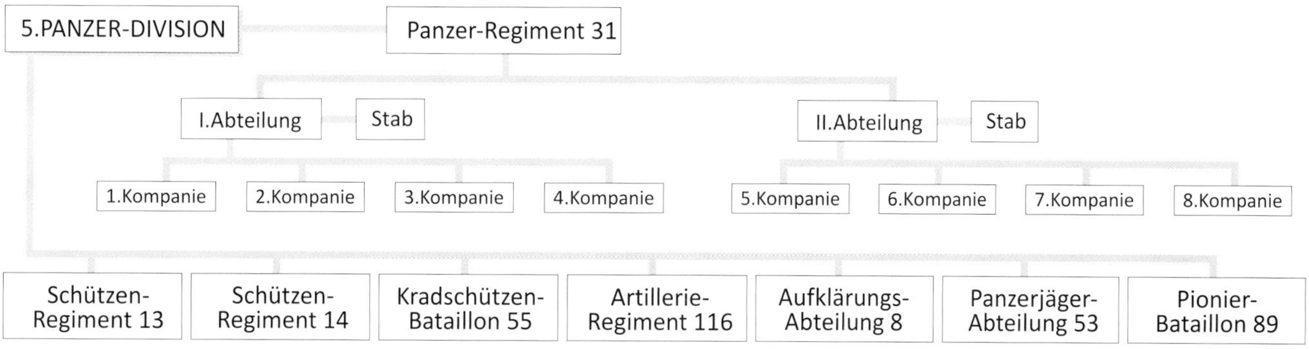

Schützen regiments were renamed as Panzergrenadier in 1942. Service units, such as medical and supply companies, were all numbered 85. Also attached to the division was schwere Infanterie-Geschütz-Kompanie 704.

The tanks of Panzer-regiment 31 did not arrive on the Eastern Front until September 1941 and within weeks the first snowfalls eventually necessitated the whitewash camouflage seen here. The interior of the hatch is decidedly darker than either the background of the unit insignia or the loader's vision port, which has been left in its original colour to display the company number. This lends credence to the suggestion that the regiment's tanks were painted in North African camouflage colours before leaving Germany. This is also discussed on page 28 of the Camouflage & Markings section of this book. This tank is an early production Pzkfw III ausf J, identified by the wooden strips on the side and lower edge of the stowage bin. These were intended to isolate the raised radio antenna from the metal of the bin when the turret was traversed. Note that the loader's port, or Klappe, has been welded shut.

9.Panzer-Division. Formed in January 1940 from 4.Leichte-Division, this formation served in the 1940 campaign in France and the Low Countries and later in the Balkans.

In June 1941 the division's Panzer-Regiment 33 was made up of two battalions, each containing one medium and two light companies. The latter were equipped with seventy-one Pzkpfw III tanks and of these, sixty were armed with the 5cm gun. As part of Panzergruppe 1 the division took part in the assault into southern Poland and the Ukraine in June 1941, reaching Annopol and Zloszow by the end of the month and it was here that the tanks of Panzer-Regiment 33 first came up against any Russian armour. In early July the division was engaged in the battles for the Stalin Line and during the middle of the month took part in the capture of Krivoy-Rog, today Kryvyi Rih in southern Ukraine, and Dniepropetrovsk. In the first weeks of September 1941 the division was involved in the crossing of the Dnieper near Kremenchug and the encirclement of the Soviet forces at Kiev, operating with just thirty-one Pzkpfw III and six Pzkpfw IV tanks. On 9 October the division was transferred to Panzergruppe 1 and took part in the drive on Moscow and the fighting around Bryansk.

In recognition of the bravery and leadership that he displayed during the November battles, Oberleutnant Georg Grüner, the commander of 1.Kompanie of Panzer-Regiment 33, was awarded the Ritterkreuz, the first soldier of the regiment to receive the medal.

The tanks of the division briefly took part in the winter defensive battles but by the end of 1941 had been withdrawn to Shchigry, about 50 kilometres east of Kursk near the present-day Ukrainian frontier.

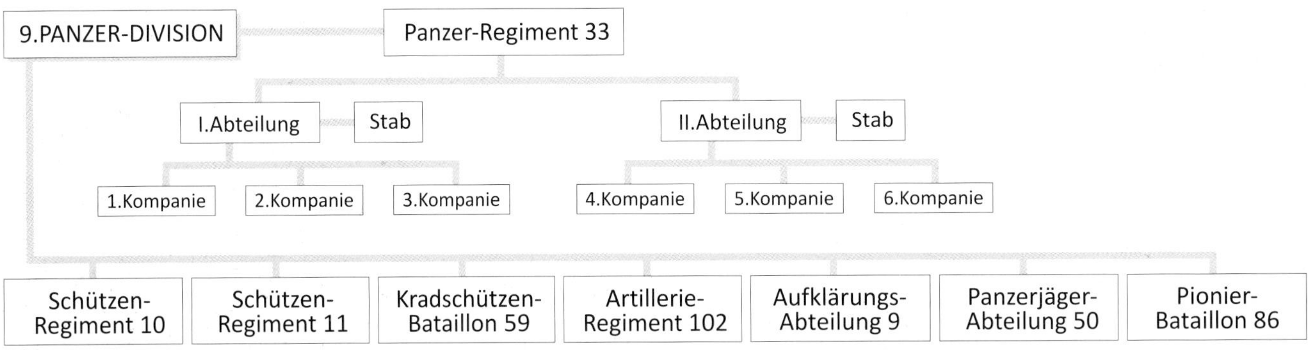

Schützen regiments were renamed as Panzergrenadier in 1942. Service units, such as medical and supply companies, were all numbered 60. Also attached to the division was Schwere Infanterie-Geschütz-Kompanie 701.

Although this photograph of a Pzkpfw III ausf F of Panzer-Regiment 33 was probably taken during the Balkan campaign, it gives a good impression of how the regiment's tanks appeared in Russia, less than two months later. The Notek light, fixed to a bracket on the hull front, was an identifying feature of this model. A number 2 is just visible in front of 33 and may have been rendered in a different colour.

A Pzkpfw III ausf F of 1.Kompanie, Panzer-Regiment 7 photographed during the early weeks of Operation Barbarossa. Note that the tank's company number has been painted onto a detachable metal rhomboid which is fixed to the hull rear. The crank port cover, just to the right of the number, and smoke candle rack were identifying features of the Pzkpfw III ausf E and ausf F models. The tanks of this regiment are also discussed on page 21 of the Camouflage & Markings section of this book.

10.Panzer-Division. Formed in 1939, this was the last of the pre-war Panzer divisions to be created and was originally organised with a full Panzer brigade of two regiments.

The division was reorganised after the French campaign to contain a single Panzer regiment but retained the staff of Panzer-Brigade 4. In June 1941 the division's Panzer-Regiment 7, commanded by Oberstleutnant Theodor Keyser, contained two battalions that were each made up of one medium and three light companies. When Operation Barbarossa commenced the regiment reported that 105 Pzkpfw III tanks were on hand and they were all armed with the 5cm gun. Subordinated to Panzergruppe 3 for Operation Barbarossa, the division took part in the advance through modern-day Belarus towards Smolensk, supported by the motorised SS-Division Reich (1).

On 25 August the division was subordinated to Panzergruppe 4 and took part in the assault on Vyazma, where two Soviet armies were surrounded and destroyed, and then the drive to Moscow.

The last available OKW situation map for December 1941 shows the division just outside Krasnogorsk, barely 10 kilometres from the Moscow city centre.

Notes

1. The division was renamed SS-Division (mot) Das Reich in May 1942.

- 10.PANZER-DIVISION
  - Stab, Panzer-Brigade 4
  - Panzer-Regiment 7
    - I.Abteilung — Stab
      - 1.Kompanie
      - 2.Kompanie
      - 3.Kompanie
      - 4.Kompanie
    - II.Abteilung — Stab
      - 5.Kompanie
      - 6.Kompanie
      - 7.Kompanie
      - 8.Kompanie
  - Schützen-Regiment 69
  - Schützen-Regiment 86
  - Kradschützen-Bataillon 10
  - Artillerie-Regiment 90
  - Aufklärungs-Abteilung 90
  - Panzerjäger-Abteilung 90
  - Pionier-Bataillon 49

Schützen regiments were renamed as Panzergrenadier in 1942. Service units, such as medical and supply companies, were all numbered 90. Also attached to the division was schwere Infanterie-Geschütz-Kompanie 706.

11.Panzer-Division. Formed in August 1940 in Germany, the division took part in the Balkan campaign. In June 1941 the division's Panzer-Regiment 15 contained two battalions, each with one medium and two light companies, and reported that seventy-one Pzkpfw III tanks were on hand of which forty-seven were armed with the 5cm gun.

As part of Panzergruppe 1 the division took part in the Bug River crossing, the tank battle at Radziechow, modern-day Radekhiv in Ukraine, and the fighting for the Stalin Line. On 20 July the tanks of the division had reached Uman and by the first week of August had linked up with elements of 101.Leichte Infanterie-Division south-east of the town. After other German units, including 16.Panzer-Division, captured Pervomaisk, about 100 kilometres further to the south-east, at least twenty-four Soviet divisions were trapped in the resulting pocket.

In late August the division was subordinated to 6.Armee for the battles around Kiev where Panzer-Regiment 15 was involved in the heavy fighting for the Dnieper bridgehead near the village of Hornostaipil. The huge distances covered and the almost constant action had taken its toll and on 5 September 1941 the division reported that just twenty-one Pzkpfw III tanks were considered operational and seven of those were replacements that had been received after June. At this time the division also reported that approximately half of its officers had been killed or wounded and the remaining units spent most of September refitting in Zhytomyr, west of Kiev.

From 11 October 1941 the division was attached to Panzergruppe 4 and fought in the double encirclement battles of Vyazma and Bryansk and the attacks towards Moscow as part of Operation Typhoon eventually advancing almost to Khimki, today an outer suburb of the capital. By the end of 1941 the division was defending the area around Gzhatsk, present-day Gagarin, about 50 kilometres west of the Napoleonic battlefield at Borodino, and remained there until the spring of 1942.

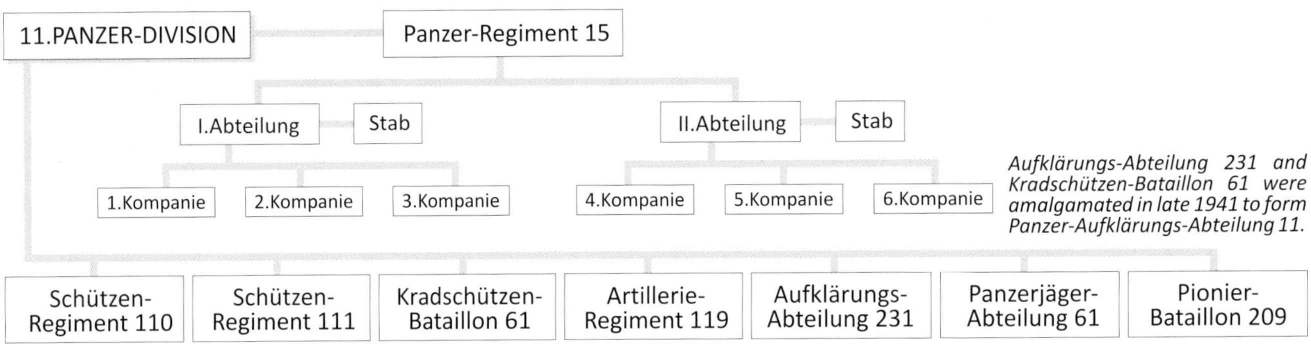

Aufklärungs-Abteilung 231 and Kradschützen-Bataillon 61 were amalgamated in late 1941 to form Panzer-Aufklärungs-Abteilung 11.

Schützen regiments were renamed as Panzergrenadier in 1942. Service units, such as medical and supply companies, were all numbered 61.

Photographed in October 1941, the vehicle closest to the camera is an upgraded Pzkpfw III ausf E or ausf F while the tank in the background is an early Pzkpfw III ausf J. Both are from 1.Kompanie, Panzer-Regiment 15 and the famous Gespentser unit symbol can be seen on the field-modified stowage box of the vehicle on the right. The tanks of this regiment are also shown in the Camouflage & Markings section on page 22.

Two Pzkpfw III ausf Gs of 3.Kompanie, Panzer-Regiment 4 undergoing repairs during the summer of 1941. The unit insignia of 13.Panzer-Division and a tactical symbol denoting the third company of a Panzer battalion is clearly visible on the hull rear above the exhaust muffler. Note the bracket on the turret rear, just below the Balkenkreuz, which supported the stowage bin.

13.Panzer-Division. Formed in October 1940, the division's Panzer-Regiment 4 was made up of two battalions, each containing one medium and two light companies.

In June 1941 the regiment reported that a full complement of seventy-one Pzkpfw III tanks were on hand and forty-four of those were equipped with the 5cm gun. Assigned to Panzergruppe 1 for Operation Barbarossa the division was initially held in reserve and crossed the River Bug on 23 June with elements of 44.Infantrie-Division near Hrubieszow in south-eastern Poland. The tanks of the division broke through the Stalin Line near Hulsk, north-west of Zhytomyr, in July 1941 and advanced into the southern Ukraine but were soon forced onto the defensive as they waited for the accompanying infantry units of III.Armeekorps to catch up. When the advance resumed the division was instrumental in capturing the city of Kremenchug on 25 August 1941 and establishing the first bridgehead across the Dnieper river at Dniepropetrovsk. At this time the regiment reported that thirty-seven Pzkpfw III and nine Pzkpfw IV tanks were considered serviceable while twenty-six of the former were in need of repair.

The division was withdrawn from the front line until late September when it took part in the attack on Mariupol on the Sea of Azov and then the offensive to take Rostov-on-Don. The tanks of Panzer-Regiment 4, supported by the infantry units of SS-Division Leibstandarte-SS Adolf Hitler, reached the outskirts of the town but were eventually forced to retire to the defensive line along the River Mius.

- 13.PANZER-DIVISION
  - Panzer-Regiment 4
    - I.Abteilung — Stab
      - 1.Kompanie
      - 2.Kompanie
      - 3.Kompanie
    - II.Abteilung — Stab
      - 7.Kompanie
      - 8.Kompanie
      - 9.Kompanie
  - Schützen-Regiment 66
  - Schützen-Regiment 93
  - Kradschützen-Bataillon 43
  - Artillerie-Regiment 13
  - Aufklärungs-Abteilung 13
  - Panzerjäger-Abteilung 13
  - Pionier-Bataillon 4

Schützen regiments were renamed as Panzergrenadier in 1942. Service units, such as medical and supply companies, were all numbered 13. The companies of II.Abteilung were numbered as shown here until early 1942.

Notes

1. Oljschaniza, mentioned in a number of German accounts in connection with this operation and described as a town, is probably the village of Olshanytsya.

14.Panzer-Division. Formed in August 1940, the division's Panzer-Regiment 36 had been detached from 4.Panzer-Division when the single regiment structure was introduced. The regiment was commanded by Oberst Curt von Jesser, an Austrian who had transferred to the Wehrmacht in 1938, and was made up of two battalions, each containing one medium company with Pzkpfw IV and two light companies equipped with Pzkpfw III tanks.

For Operation Barbarossa the division was attached to Panzergruppe 1, the main strike force of Heeresgruppe Süd. On 22 June 1941 the division moved into Soviet territory through Ustyluh on the modern-day Polish border and by 1 July had reached Rovno, today Rivne in western Ukraine. Within nine days the division had advance a further 100 kilometres to capture Novohrad-Volynskyi, formerly Zwiahel, a forward element of the Stalin Line.

From there the tanks of Panzer-Regiment 36 pushed forward to Bila Tserkva, south-west of Kiev, and after clearing the forests north of Tarashcha (1) the division reached Bohuslaw on 26 July 1941, taking the town on the following day. From there the division raced south towards Pervomaisk in an effort to trap the Soviet units fighting around Uman. Once the encirclement was completed the Panzers were sent to the south-east, taking part in the capture of Kryvyi Rih, formerly Krivoy Rog, on 14 August 1941 and the battle for Dniepropetrovsk, which lasted until 10 September. Just days prior to this the regiment had reported that forty-nine Pzkpfw III and fifteen Pzkpfw IV tanks were fully operational and although seventeen of the former had been completely destroyed, only nine tanks were in need of repair.

14.Panzer-Division remained in the Dniepropetrovsk area which was the scene of heavy fighting until 10 October when the attack on Mariupol on the Sea of Azov began. From Sunday, 19 October 1941 the division was involved in the attempts to take Rostov-on-Don and although some forward elements actually entered the city on the following Wednesday, the Germans were driven out by a series of strong Russian counterattacks.

By 1 December the division had withdrawn to the Mius River defensive line where it remained until the spring of 1942.

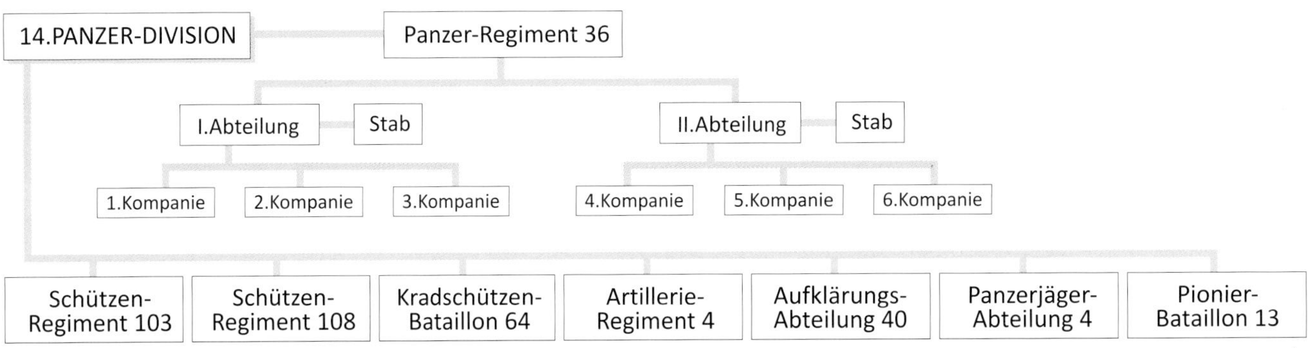

Schützen regiments were renamed as Panzergrenadier in 1942. Service units, such as medical and supply companies, were all numbered 4.

Although it is not possible to identify the unit to which this late production Pzkpfw III ausf G belongs with any certainty, the numbers are similar to those seen on some tanks of Panzer-Regiment 36. The tanks of this regiment are also discussed on page 27 of the Camouflage & Markings section.

A Panzerbefehlswagen III ausf H, identified by the additional armour on the hull front, from one of the divisions of Panzergruppe 1 photographed in southern Ukraine. The white Panzer rhomboid symbol on the loader's vision port suggests that this tank was attached to a company headquarters.

16.Panzer-Division. This formation was created in August 1940 by combining the units of 16.Infanterie-Division with Panzer-Regiment 2 which had been detached from 1.Panzer-Division.

In June 1941 Panzer-Regiment 2 was made up of two battalions, each containing one medium company and two light companies. Just prior to the invasion of the Soviet Union the division reported that a total of seventy-one Pzkpfw III tanks were on hand with the light companies, of which forty-eight were fitted with the 5cm gun. Commanded by Oberstleutnant Rudolf Sieckenius, the regiment was famous for its aristocratic make up and Berndt Freytag von Loringhoven, who served with the second company, recalled in his memoirs that many of the officers were addressed by their titles rather than their army rank.

As part of Panzergruppe 1 the division followed 11.Panzer-Division across the Soviet border between Sokal and Chervonohrad on 24 June 1941 and was immediately engaged the heavy fighting for Kremenets, Starokostyantyniv and Lyubar which was part of the Stalin Line. The division took part in the Battle of Uman but was so roughly handled by the Soviets that the reconnaissance units were almost wiped out and the remnants were returned to Germany. On 3 August the division captured the bridge over the Southern Bug River, or Pivdennyi Buh, at Pervomaisk and pushed on to the Black Sea coast, taking Nikolayev on 16 August after which 16.Panzer-Division was withdrawn from the front.

At that time Panzer-Regiment 2 could field just twenty-six of the seventy-one Pzkpfw III tanks that had begun the campaign and the division reported that seventy tanks of all types, including four command vehicles, had been completely destroyed since June.

In September the division returned to the fighting and took part in the assault out of the Dnieper bridgehead at Kremenchug, capturing Lubny on 14 September and helping to complete the encirclement of Kiev. The division was involved in the advance to Rostov-on-Don but the onset of winter and a series of Russian counterattacks forced the survivors of 16.Panzer-Division back to the Mius River defensive positions, at first to the town of Matveyev Kurgan on the present-day Ukrainian border and then to Makiivka outside Donetsk.

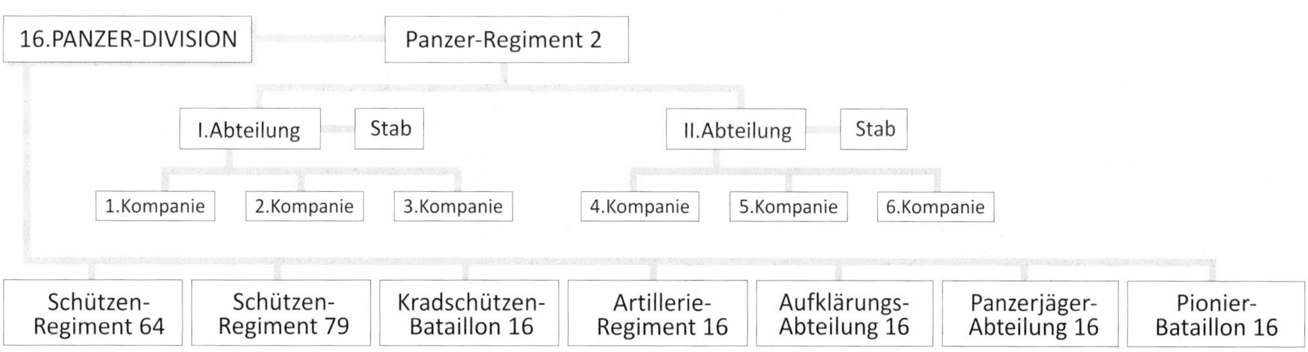

Schützen regiments were renamed as Panzergrenadier in 1942. Service units, such as medical and supply companies, were all numbered 16.

Notes

1. Contrary to some accounts Weber did not lead the division at the commencement of Barbarossa. He took over on 24 June 1941 when the original commander, General Hans-Jürgen von Arnim, was wounded.

2. The OKW situation map for 1 December 1941 actually shows 17.Panzer-Division spread out around the small town of Konchinka, about 60 kilometres closer to Moscow. The briefest glance at the map shows how exposed the remnants of 17.Panzer-Division were at this time with a number of Russian infantry and armoured units positioned between them and the line held by the other units of XXXXIII.Armeekorps.

17.Panzer-Division. Formed in November 1940, the division's Panzer-Regiment 39, commanded by Oberst Kurt Cuno, was created from the training and replacement battalions of Panzer-Regiment 4 and Panzer-Regiment 33. In June 1941 the regiment was made up of three battalions. Each battalion contained one medium company and two light companies and a number of the Pzkpfw III and Pzkpfw IV tanks were Tauchpanzer submersible vehicles. At that time the division reported that a total of 106 Pzkpfw III tanks were on hand, all armed with the 5cm gun.

Although many accounts suggest that the submersible tanks of Panzer-Regiment 39 were used to cross the River Bug on the morning of 22 June 1941, no less an authority than Generaloberst Guderian recalled that only the tanks of Panzer-Regiment 18 were employed in the specialised role for which they were designed. From the Bug River crossings the division advanced towards the area south of Minsk and by the last week of June had linked up with units of Panzergruppe 3. In early July the tanks of Panzer-Regiment 39 took part in the battles fought between Bialystok and Minsk where the division claimed to have destroyed over 100 Soviet tanks in a single action near Orsha. In August and September the division took part in the defensive battles south of Smolensk where the acting commander, Generalmajor Karl Ritter von Weber, was mortally wounded (1). In fact, the division had been involved in some of the heaviest fighting of the campaign up to this point and on 10 September 1941 reported that seventy-two tanks of all types had been completely destroyed including thirty-nine Pzkpfw III tanks, the backbone of the Panzer regiment. In early October the division fought in the battles around Bryansk in the preliminary operations of the general assault on Moscow and eventually reached Tula, about 180 kilometres south of the Soviet capital (2).

When the massive Soviet counter offensive began of 5 December the division was pushed back over 120 kilometres in just three days and eventually took up defensive positions north-east of Orel, present-day Oryol, where it remained until the summer of 1942.

- 17.PANZER-DIVISION
  - Panzer-Regiment 39
    - I.Abteilung – Stab
      - 1.Kompanie
      - 2.Kompanie
      - 3.Kompanie
    - II.Abteilung – Stab
      - 4.Kompanie
      - 5.Kompanie
      - 6.Kompanie
    - III.Abteilung – Stab
      - 7.Kompanie
      - 8.Kompanie
      - 9.Kompanie
  - Schützen-Regiment 40
  - Schützen-Regiment 63
  - Kradschützen-Bataillon 17
  - Artillerie-Regiment 27
  - Aufklärungs-Abteilung 27
  - Panzerjäger-Abteilung 27
  - Pionier-Bataillon 27

Schützen regiments were renamed as Panzergrenadier in 1942. Service units, such as medical and supply companies, were all numbered 27.

A Pzkpfw III ausf G of Panzer-Regiment 39 identified by the official formation insignia of 17.Panzer-Division on the hull side next to the Balkenkreuz. Just visible in the original print of this photograph, on the left-hand side of the hull rear plate, is a white rhomboid tactical symbol and a number, which is unfortunately illegible but appears to end in 0. This vehicle is also shown and discussed on page 27 of the Camouflage & Markings section of this book.

Photographed during a training session, this Tauchpanzer conversion of Panzer-Regiment 18 is based on a Pzkpfw III ausf H. The white number 100 almost certainly indicates the commander of the regiment's 1.Kompanie. The tanks of this unit are also shown in the Camouflage & Markings section on page 23.

18.Panzer-Division. Formed in October 1940, it was expected that this division would take part in the invasion of Britain and it originally contained four battalions which were later combined into two Panzer regiments, largely equipped with Tauchpanzer submersible tanks.

In June 1941 the division's Panzer-Regiment 18 was made up of three battalions and each battalion contained one medium company and two light companies. The latter were equipped with a total of 106 Pzkpfw III tanks but only fifteen of these were fitted with the 5cm gun. Records regarding the actual number of Pzkpfw III and Pzkpfw IV Tauchpanzer do not seem to have survived the war. In addition the division retained the staff of Panzer-Brigade 18 and this unit operated at least two Panzerbefehlswagen III command tanks which had been fitted with deep wading attachments.

Attached to Panzergruppe 2 the division crossed the Bug River in the early hours of 22 June 1941, using the Panzer regiment's submersible tanks, near the village of Pratulin, north-east of Brest-Litovsk. By the end of the month the tanks of 18.Panzer-Division were at Minsk, today the capital of Belarus, and from there advanced to Borisov, modern-day Barysaw, and crossed the Berezina River. In July the division took part in the battles for Smolensk and Roslavl and by the end of August was involved in the defensive fighting along the Desna River on the Russian frontier. Unlike many of the other German armoured formations, Panzer-Regiment 18 had been fortunate in receiving twenty replacement Pzkpfw III tanks after the beginning of the campaign but the immense distances had taken a toll on all the vehicles and on 9 September 1941, the division reported that 114 tanks of all types were under repair.

On 30 September 1941 the German advance was resumed and within five days the division had pushed forward to Karachev, 50 kilometres south-east of Bryansk, crossing four rivers in the process.

In October 1941, as part of Panzergruppe 2, the division took part in the advance towards Moscow. Many accounts state that the division reached Tula, south of Moscow, but the OKW situation map of 1 December 1941 shows the positions of 18.Panzer-Division around the village of Boryatino on the Moscow to Voronezh road about 100 kilometres further to the south and it is doubtful that any further progress was made.

In the face of the Russian counteroffensive to save Moscow the division was able to hold on to its positions until 14 December 1941 but eventually retreated towards the west, reaching Mtsensk on the Zusha river, north-east of Oryol on Christmas Day.

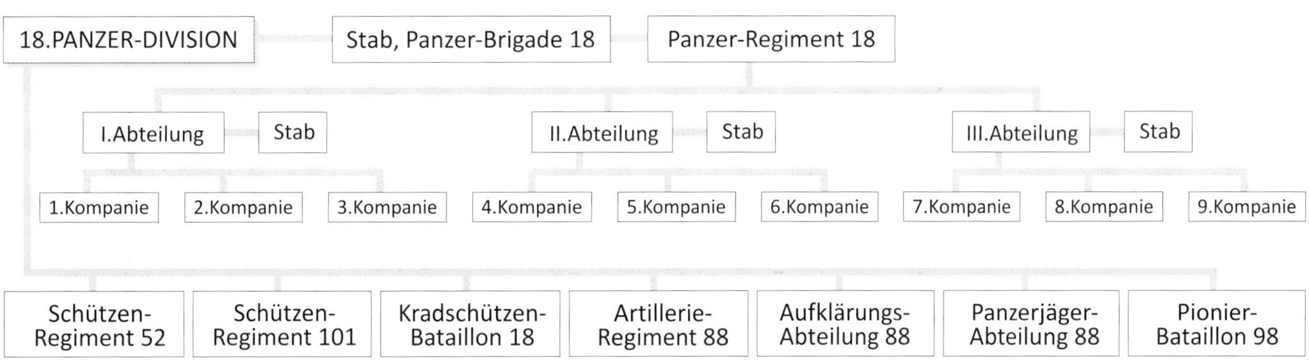

Schützen regiments were renamed as Panzergrenadier in 1942. Service units, such as medical and supply companies, were all numbered 88.

Panzer-Regiment 203. Formed in July 1941 with captured French armoured vehicles, the regiment was hurriedly re-equipped with forty-five Pzkpfw II, seventy-one Pzkpfw III, twenty Pzkpfw IV and six Panzerbefehlswagen III command tanks and rushed to the Eastern Front in December. The regiment was attached to I.Armeekorps but acted as an armoured reserve for 18.Armee fighting around Leningrad. Withdrawn from the front in February 1942, Panzer-Regiment 203 was eventually disbanded.

Panzer-Abteilung (Fl) 100. Containing three companies, this battalion was equipped with forty-two Flammpanzer II flamethrower tanks and five Pzkpfw III, the latter probably used as command and control vehicles. During the battles on the Eastern Front the three companies were allocated to 18.Panzer-Division, 17.Panzer-Division and Infanterie-Regiment Grossdeutschland. An interesting photograph of a Pzkpfw III of 2.Kompanie, numbered 201, suggests that the tanks carried the unit insignia of the formations to which they were attached. In November 1941 the remaining tanks were handed over to Panzer-Regiment 18 and the battalion was disbanded.

Panzer-Abteilung (Fl) 101. The battalion was organised and equipped identically to Panzer-Abteilung (Fl) 100 was attached to XXXIX.Armeekorps of Panzergruppe 3 and then to XXXXI.Armeekorps and took part in the fighting for Kalinin. On 8 December 1941 the battalion was disbanded and the remaining personnel incorporated into the newly-formed Panzer-Regiment 24.

Panzer-Abteilung zbV 40. Formed in March 1940, this independent battalion was lead by Oberstleutnant Ernst Volkheim who had commanded an A7V tank unit during the last months of 1918 and taken part in the First Battle of Villers-Bretonneux. The battalion's first, second and third companies were made up from drafts from Panzer-Regimenten 6, 35 and 15 respectively. The battalion famously took part in the fighting in Norway in 1940, operating three Neubaufahrzeug Panzer IV heavy tanks.

In June 1941 the battalion took part in Operation Silver Fox, a joint German-Finnish assault intended to capture the Soviet port of Murmansk. The battalion staff and 2.Kompanie were attached to Höheres Kommando zbV XXXVI and supported an assault made by SS-Kampfgruppe Nord towards modern-day Kandalaksha, situated on the northern end of the White Sea, while 1.Kompanie, as part of Gebirgs-Armeekorps Norwegen, pushed across the Norwegian border directly towards Murmansk. The battalion's 3.Kompanie was subordinated to an ad-hoc Finnish army formation at Raatevaara, much further to the south around Lake Ladoga. The exact make up of the battalion at this time is not known but it has been suggested that the second and third companies contained ten Pzkpfw III tanks each and nine vehicles have so far been confirmed by photographic evidence, including four early ausf D models. In December 1941 the three companies reported that eight Pzkpfw III, seven Pzkpfw I and a single Pzkpfw II light tank were on hand.

Notes

1. These tanks were actually from Panzerzug Horstmann which was temporarily attached to the battalion and at least one was destroyed in Norway.

Our photograph shows an early production PzKfw III ausf H towing a Pzkpfw III ausf.J from the muddy riverbank near Kiestinki, modern-day Kestenga in northern Russia. Both vehicles are from 3.Kompanie, Panzer-Abteilung zbV 40 and are typical of the company's tanks which all seemd to lack the turret stowage bin or Rommelkiste. The application of the large turret numbers was also consistent throughout the company.

This Pzkpfw III ausf E has the early commander's cupola and the 3.7cm KwK 36 L/45 gun. Note the bolted-on machine-gun mount, the rain guard over the driver's visor and the two large towing eyes fixed to the hull front. On the subsequent model, the Pzkpfw III ausf F, cast armoured cowls were fitted over the cooling apertures for the steering brakes next to the headlights. The drive sprocket and rear idler are the early types and were referred to by the drawing numbers B 9201 and B 9207 respectively. When tanks with this early turret were retro-fitted with the stowage bin a bracket was needed to hold it in place and it can be seen here just behind the turret side access doors.

As mentioned elsewhere, the first models of the Pzkpfw III were essentially development vehicles and although a handful served with Panzer-Abteilung zbV 40 during the early stages of Operation Barbarossa in northern Russia I have chosen to concentrate on the later versions here which, by 1941, were far more numerous. However, many of the features of the original designs became standard in the mass production models and they deserve at least a brief mention. Every tank was identified by a Fahrgestellnummer, or chassis number, usually abbreviated to Fgst Nr., and these can sometimes be seen in contemporary photographs. As they are a certain means of identifying a model or version I have included them here as they related to a particular production batch. For reasons of space I have not included the modification and placement of many small details such as lifting hooks, tool clasps and hinges and the following is intended to be a spotter's guide to enable the modeller and interested reader to differentiate between the models of the Pzkpfw III that were in service in 1941.

Pzkpfw III ausf A. Although similar in silhouette to the later models, this version is easily distinguished by its five large roadwheels and two return rollers. Just ten of these vehicles were assembled in 1937 by Daimler-Benz, with Fgst Nr. 60101 to 60110, of which eight were fitted with the 3.7cm KwK 36 L/45 gun (1). The armour thickness ranged from 5mm to 15mm and the design of the turret was based on that of the Pzkpfw IV but with a smaller turret ring diameter of 152 centimetres. The tank's turret, with minor modifications, became a standard feature of the Pzkpfw III design and its size would eventually bring a halt to development from 1943 when larger-calibre weapons were need. A simple drum-style cupola with direct vision slots was fitted to the turret and the side access doors were made in one piece. An unknown number of Pzkpfw III ausf A tanks were used in Poland in 1939 as command vehicles after which they were relegated to training roles.

Pzkpfw III ausf B. The hull design was similar to the Pzkpfw III ausf A with some minor modifications including new engine exhaust mufflers and a redesigned driver's vision port. The simple drum cupola of the turret was replaced by the version used in the production of the Pzkpfw IV ausf A, which had a higher profile, and the side access doors were slightly more rounded. The radio antenna bracket on the starboard side of the hull was moved forward. The drive sprocket and rear idler were those fitted to the earlier model but the large roadwheels were replaced by a leaf spring suspension with two bogies supporting a total of eight small roadwheels and the number of return rollers was increased to three. A total of fifteen of these tanks, numbered from 60201 to 60215, were built in 1937 (2) and a small number served in the Polish campaign.

Pzkpfw III ausf C. The hull of this model was almost identical to the Pzkpfw III ausf B with the exception of the exhaust mufflers which were modified to accommodate a smoke candle discharger on the rear hull. The suspension was redesigned so that the first and last pairs

Notes

1. The two unarmed tanks were presumably used as test vehicles.
2. Five of these were used in 1938 as development vehicles in the Sturmgeschütz assault gun programme.

Notes

1. I have included the official drawing numbers here as an easy reference and they are shown and described as such in the accompanying photographs. I have deliberately omitted the prefix 021, which was applied to all, as this referred to the Pzkpfw III.
2. To avoid damage to the rubber roadwheels, strict orders were issued that this speed was not to be exceeded.
3. This cover, or Tarnkappe, is present on Fgst Nr. 60428 but missing on some vehicles with higher numbers. It should be noted that most modifications were introduced at slightly different times by manufacturers.
4. The FuG 5, or Funkgerät 5, was the standard radio installed in all German tanks with a range of about 2 to 3 kilometres. The FuG 2 was commonly fitted in company command vehicles and offered the capability to listen on one frequency while transmitting and receiving on another.
5. Fgst Nr. 61314, assembled by Henschel, and Fgst Nr. 61225, built by Famo, still had this feature.

of wheels were mounted on short springs which sat parallel to the ground while the second and third pairs of wheels were carried on one long leaf spring. The drive sprocket, rear idler and return rollers were the same as those fitted to the earlier models. A total of fifteen Pzkpfw III ausf C were built, with Fgst Nr. 60301 to 60315, and a small number took part in the Polish campaign.

Pzkpfw III ausf D. This model was the final attempt to rectify the problems experienced with the leaf spring suspension. The drive sprocket, rear idler and return rollers of the Pzkpfw III ausf A were retained and the second and third pairs of wheels remained unchanged from the Pzkpfw III ausf B design, but the short leaf springs for the first and fourth pairs of roadwheels were now mounted at an angle. The amount of support this arrangement provided was minimal and future models would feature a completely redesigned suspension layout. A new commander's cupola with five vision slots and protected by a 30mm thick armour belt was fitted to this model and would remain a feature of production until part-way through the Pzkpfw III ausf G series. Daimler-Benz assembled thirty of these tanks and although they were officially withdrawn from front-line service in February 1940, at least four Pzkpfw III ausf D served with Panzer-Abteilung zbV 40 in northern Russia in 1941. The chassis numbers for the entire production run were 60221 to 60225 and 60316 to 60340.

Pzkpfw III ausf E. This was essentially the first mass-produced version of the tank and featured a completely different suspension based on a torsion bar system developed by Professor Ferdinand Porsche. In place of the complicated and somewhat delicate leaf springs, six roadwheels were each fixed to the hull by a lever which was in turn held on a steel bar that ran across the width of the tank. Large shock absorbers, the early B 9209 version, were attached to the first and last lever on each side (1). The flexibility and sturdiness of this arrangement allowed the chassis to absorb considerably more shock and although the armour thickness of the turret and hull front was increased to 30mm, with a commensurate increase in weight, a speed of 40 kilometres per hour could be attained by the installation of the more powerful Maybach HL120TR engine (2). Three return rollers were placed above the roadwheels and a new drive sprocket, B 92011, and rear idler, B 9207, were introduced. The hull sides were now constructed of a single metal sheet and the space left by the omission of the leaf spring suspension components meant that an escape hatch could be included between the roadwheels and return rollers. In addition to the suspension and the internal changes, the simple flap over the driver's vision slot was replaced by a two-part armoured visor with a large rain guard and the single-piece access doors on the turret sides were replaced by double doors equipped with vision slots and pistol ports which opened outwards. The two signal ports incorporated into the turret roof on earlier models were retained and the left port was protected by a prominent armoured cover which could also act as a signal light. This cover may have been deleted from very late production vehicles and it was certainly removed from any vehicles returned to the factories for repair (3). The square-shaped pistol ports on the turret rear were replaced by metal cones. On the right side of the hull a 2-metre antenna was held in an extended mount which could pivot down to 95 degrees to sit in a wooden trough. This was a feature of the subsequent models described here. In tanks allocated to company or platoon commanders the FuG 2 radio was fitted in place of the more common FuG 5 set (4). Although the shape of the rear hull changed slightly, the starter crank cover and smoke candle discharger of the Pzkpfw III ausf D were retained.

The production model of the Pzkpfw III ausf E was armed with the 3.7cm main gun but from late 1940, as part of the Umbewaffnung programme, many were retrofitted with the 5cm weapon and a number of new features (see below). A total of ninety-six Pzkpfw III ausf E were built by Daimler-Benz, Henschel and MAN, with Fgst Nr. 60401 to 60496, and many were still in service in 1941.

Pzkpfw III ausf F. Although this tank was fitted with a slightly more powerful Maybach HL 120 TRM engine and a modified engine cooling system, the early production vehicles were almost identical to the Pzkpfw III ausf E and the two models are often difficult to differentiate in photographs. Very early in the production run two armoured cowls were fitted over the cooling apertures for the steering brakes on the upper hull front. From about March 1940 a shot deflector, which protected the base of the turret, was installed on the hull roof. This was fabricated in three sections and bolted internally. In the same month a Notek light was mounted on the front left track guard and the tail light on the same guard was replaced by a convoy light. A rectangular hole was cut into the hinged fender to accommodate the convoy light. In May 1940 the rubber tyres of the roadwheels were increased in width from 75mm to 95mm and some tanks seen in contemporary photographs have a mixture of both. The Tarnkappe on the turret roof was dropped by some manufacturers very early in the production run but seems to have been retained by others until at least mid-1940 (5). It was reported that the tracks were

liable to hit the shock absorber mounts and in September 1940, in an effort to rectify the problem, the forward return roller was moved closer the drive sprocket. An interesting feature of the Pzkpfw III ausf F tanks completed by Henschel seems to be the lack of a radio operator's vision port on the right side of the hull. Due to a delay in the delivery of armoured components a number of vehicles, perhaps as many as ninety-six, were completed after July 1940 with the external gun mantlet, B 39033, and 5cm weapon intended for the Pzkpfw III ausf H model (A). A total of 435 Pzkpfw III ausf F tanks were assembled, numbered from 61001 to 61650, and they served in France, the Balkans, North Africa and Russia.

Pzkpfw III ausf G. This model was a development of the Pzkpfw III ausf F with the major difference being an increase in the thickness of the rear armour from 21mm to 30mm. The first fifty tanks were assembled with the 3.7cm KwK 36 L/45 gun before the 5cm KwK 38 L/42 weapon was introduced which was fitted to the remaining 550 production vehicles (1). A Notek night-driving light (B) was mounted on the front left track guard and the tail light was replaced by a convoy light as mentioned for the Pzkpfw III ausf F. The partitioned driver's visor was replaced by a pivoting version (C), behind which a 90mm thick glass block protected the driver, and a twin periscope was installed. At the hull rear an armoured cover was provided for the smoke candle discharger. Several modifications introduced into the Pzkpfw III ausf F, which was still in production, were also incorporated into the Pzkpfw III ausf G. These included the increase in width of the roadwheel tyres from 75mm to 95mm and the placement of the first return roller closer to the drive sprocket.

In June 1940 the ventilation fan was moved to the centre of the turret roof and on some tanks a circular plate covered the hole that had already been cut to the left of the commander's cupola, B9292, was introduced (D). This cupola featured vertically opening vision slots and was identical to the version fitted to the Pzkpfw IV. A rudimentary direction indicator, or Richtungszeiger, was located directly in front of the forward vision slot.

At about the same time, face-hardened plates of 30mm thickness (E) were bolted onto the hull glacis, the hull front and hull rear. A number of tanks were assembled with the bolts fixed in place before the armour plates were available and were issued to units in this state. Although images of these tanks are rare, as the plates were usually retro-fitted in the field, they can be seen from time to time.

Late in the production run the widened suspension was fitted with the later drive sprocket (F) and rear idler (G), B 39008 and B 39004, and shock absorbers, B 39006. A total of 600 Pzkpfw III ausf Gs were assembled, with Fgst Nr. 65001 to 65950, and were employed in France, the Balkans, North Africa and Russia before production ended in late 1940 (2).

Notes

1. The last tanks with the 3.7cm guns were built by Alkett in August and September 1940.
2. The blocks of numbers allocated for armoured vehicle production were usually more than required for security reasons.

Notes

1. The Heereswaffenamt, or army ordnance office, was responsible for the design, testing, development and acceptance of all weaponry including armoured vehicles.

2. Stowage bins were authorised for all Pzkpfw III tanks by an order of 23 April 1941. The modification of Pzkpfw III ausf F and G vehicles for tropical service began in January 1941 and involved cutting large holes in the rear deck hatch lids, which were then protected by armoured covers, and increasing the cooling fan speed.

The Umbewaffnung programme. By 25 September 1940, the Heereswaffenamt (1) had determined that approximately 1,200 Pzkpfw III tanks already in service would need to be upgraded to something approaching the standard of the Pzkpfw III ausf H, that was just about to come into service, and the Pzkpfw III ausf J which was still in the development stage.

The most important modifications included the installation of the 5cm gun and external mantlet, the fitting of additional armour, referred to as Zusatzpanzerung, the widening of the suspension and the replacement of the shock absorbers (A) and torsion bars with newer versions.

About half the tanks in question would need all the modifications listed while the remainder would only require an upgrade to their suspension. It was anticipated that the modifications would be completed by March 1941. In addition to the modifications mentioned here, many tanks were fitted with Gepäckkasten or stowage bins (B) and the armoured covers of the so-called Tropen air intakes (C) (2).

It should also be noted that not all the early model tanks were fitted with all the desired modifications and it is common to see a mixture of early and late features. Examples of these are shown in the Camouflage & Markings section.

Pzkpfw III ausf H. The development of this model began in January 1939 and as it was originally intended that this would be the first of the Pzkpfw III tanks armed with the 5cm gun, a total of 759 were ordered. But as the newer gun was progressively retro-fitted to earlier models the need for the Pzkpfw III ausf H, which was really an interim variant, was diminished and just 308 were produced. The most notable difference was the addition of 30mm armour plates to the hull front and rear, held in place by large bolts (D), providing protection against any anti-tank gun in service in 1941. The increase in weight was compensated for by widening the suspension and fitting the tank with 400mm wide Kgs 61/400/120 tracks (E). The drive sprocket, rear idler and shock absorbers, as fitted to the later production versions of the Pzkpfw III ausf G, were standard on this model. Two small distinguishing features of the Pzkpfw III ausf H were the wooden strips added to the turret stowage bin (F) that prevented the radio antenna from coming into contact with the metal box and the crank handle cover which now opened upwards (G). The complex and problematic Variorex pre-selective transmission, that had been trialled on earlier models, was replaced by a new Maybach version and the torsion bars were strengthened. Production versions of the Pzkpfw III ausf H were numbered in the 660001 to 66650 series.

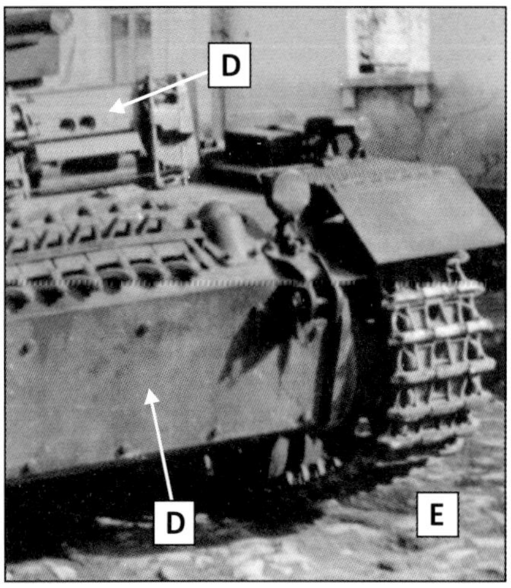

Based on an early production model Pzkpfw III ausf G, this Tauchpanzer conversion has the early internal gun mantlet and 3.7cm gun but has been fitted with the later cupola, drawing B 9292, and a stowage bin. Note that the waterproof covering for the hull machine gun is still in place while the cover for the main gun appears to have been cut away.

Pzkpfw III ausf J. This version was the final development model of the Pzkpfw III tank, subsequent models being variations, and is easily identifiable by the 50mm front plate with a redesigned driver's visor and Kugelblende machine-gun mount. The smoke candle dischargers were dropped from production and the rear hull was made up of two flat armour plates above a deflector for the exhaust. The Tropen air intake system, with its distinctive armoured covers, was standard on this version as were the single-piece inspection hatches on the hull front. The hull side plates were extended at the front providing integral towing eyes which obviated the need for the bolt-on versions of earlier models. Although the wider suspension was standard on this model a number of photographs exist of Pzkpfw III tanks fitted with the earlier style drive sprocket and rear idlers. The first Pzkpfw III ausf J tanks left the assembly lines in early 1941 and all the tanks that took part in Operation Barbarossa were armed with the 5cm KwK L/42 gun, arriving in Russia with Panzer-Regiment 3 and Panzer-Regiment 31 in September.

Tauchpanzer III. Between June and October 1940, in anticipation of Operation Sealion, the planned invasion of south-eastern England, a number of Pzkpfw III and Pzkpfw IV tanks were modified to operate underwater. Referred to as Tauchpanzer, or diving tanks, the hatches and other openings were sealed with a special waterproof compound and the gap between the turret and hull was covered with an inflatable rubber ring held in place by metal brackets. Similar waterproof covers were fitted to the commander's cupola, the gun mantlet and the hull machine gun. The tank's engine intakes were closed with rubber seals and the modified exhausts were fitted with non-return valves to prevent water flooding the engine. The crew, and engine, were supplied with air by an 18-metre long hose which was attached to a large circular buoy floating on the surface. An extended air intake, approximately 1.5 metres high, was fitted to the buoy and this would, in calm seas, be sufficient to deal with the waves on the day of the invasion. In the event of the waterproof seals or hose failing, each vehicle was fitted with a number of pumps and, with the aid of these, the tank was capable of remaining submerged for up to twenty minutes at a depth of 15 metres. Once ashore, the commander was able to remove the rubber seals and covers from inside the tank by triggering the small explosive charges that were attached to each.

A total of 160 Pzkpfw III ausf F, G and H tanks and eight Panzerbefehlswagen III ausf E command vehicles were converted and they were intended to accompany the first assault wave (1). When the invasion of Britain was abandoned the tanks were allocated to the divisions that were to take part in Operation Barbarossa and this is discussed further in the unit histories. On 22 June 1941, near the village of Pratulin, some 12 kilometres north-west of Brest in modern-day Belarus, the Tauchpanzer submersible tanks of Panzer-Regiment 18 crossed the Bug River into Soviet territory. By this time the hose and buoy arrangement that supplied fresh air to the submerged tanks had been replaced by a simple snorkel system that limited the operational depth to just 4 metres. This was perfectly sufficient for the relatively calm waters of even a major river and the crossing was a complete success (2).

Notes

1. The plan's weakness lay in the fact that the tanks were required to embark from vessels that would need to come to a complete stop in relatively shallow water, while every gun in the area could be brought to bear on them.
2. The honour of driving the first German submersible tank into action goes to the regiment's Stabsfeldwebel Helmuth Wierschin, a platoon commander with the second company.

Dragon Models Ltd
B1-10/F., 603-609 Castle Peak Rd,
Kong Nam Industrial Building,
Tsuen Wan, N. T., Hong Kong
www.dragon-models.com

Tamiya Inc
Shizuoka City, Japan
www.tamiya.com

Milicast Models
9 Rannoch Street,
Battlefield,
Glasgow G44 4DF
www.milicast.com

First To Fight
ul. Jana Bulhaka 11,
01-472, Warszawa,
Poland
www.wrzesien1939.pl/

Miniart
144 B Kharkivske Highway,
02091 Kiev,
Ukraine
www.miniart-models.com

Panzerart
Ul. Borowa 7,
41-260 Slakow,
Poland
www.panzerart.pl

Royal Model
Via E. Montale, 19-95030,
Pedara, Italy
www.royalmodel.com

Italeri S.p.A.
via Pradazzo 6/b,
40012 Calderara di Reno, Bologna, Italy
www.italeri.com

JK Resin
Cajkovského 22,
74601 Opava, Czech Republic

Hauler
Jan Sobotka,
Moravská 38, 620 00 Brno,
Czech Republic
www.hauler.cz

Voyager
Room 501, No.411 4th Village,
SPC Jinshan District, Shanghai 200540,
P.R.China
www.voyagermodel.com

Griffon Model
Suite 501, Bldg 01, 418 Middle Longpan Rd,
Nanjing, China
www.griffonmodel.com

Aber
ul. Jalowcowa 15, 40-750 Katowice, Poland
www.aber.net.pl

E.T. Model
www.etmodeller.com

Friulmodel
H 8142. Urhida, Nefelejcs u. 2., Hungary
www.friulmodel.hu

Modelkasten
Chiyoda-ku Kanda, Nishiki-Cho 1-7, Tokyo,
Japan
www.modelkasten.com
Very difficult to navigate but worthwhile.

Black Dog
Petr Polanka,
Letecká 549,
Libcice nad Vltavou,252 66,
Czech Republic
www.blackdog.cz

Spade Ace Models
This company may have closed but the tracks are avaialble from Sincere Hobby in Hong Kong.
www.sincerehobby.com

Eduard Model Accessories
Mirova 170, 435 21 Obrnice,
Czech Republic
www.eduard.com

Master Club
www.masterclub.ru
It appears that this firm is closely associated with Armour35, a Russsian mail-order firm.

RB Model
Powstancow Wlkp.29B,
64-360 Zbaszyn,
Poland
www.rbmodel.com

M Workshop Singapore
91 Bencoolen St, Sunshine Plaza 01-58,
Singapore
www.themworkshop.com

Zvezda (Zvezda-America)
www.zvezda-usa.com
Note that the Russian catalogue is not the same as the US version.

OzArmour
P.O Box 51,
Burpengary, QLD, 4505,
Australia
www.ozarmour.com.au

Kaizen
Like many Chinese companies this is hard to pin down to an exact location. The tracks are available from MS Models Japan, a firm for which I can personally vouch.
www.msmodelswebshop.jp

Mike Tipping Models
West Gate House,
94 Main Road,
Gedling
Nottingham NG4 3HG
www.miketippingmodels.co.uk

In writing this book I referred extensively to *Panzerkampfwagen III Ausf E, F, G und H* by the late Thomas L. Jentz and Hilary Louis Doyle. Other invaluable resources were are Thomas Jentz's Panzertruppen books, which I would recommend to any reader with an interest in German armour, and *Achtung Panzer No 2 Panzerkampfwagen III*. Although the latter is for the most part written in Japanese, Philip Greenwood's English captions and the brilliant illustrations of Mitsuru Bitoh and Tomioka Yoshikatsu make everything clear. I should also acknowledge the work of Martin Block and the late Ron Klages whose research on unit histories and vehicle allocations would fill many volumes. I would like to thank the modellers who graciously allowed me to publish the images of their work and I must make special mention of Jan Zdiarsky from Eduard Model Accessories, Freddie Leung of Dragon Models and the crew at E.T. Models who all helped enormously. As always, I am indebted to Karl Berne, Valeri Polokov and J.Howard Parker for their invaluable assistance with the photographs and period insignia.

Pzkpfw III ausf J tanks from the headquarters of 6.Kompanie, Panzer-Regiment 3 photographed in Russia. This regiment, attached to 2.Panzer-Division, was refitting when Operation Barbarossa commenced and was allocated a significant number of these later production models, the first examples of which left the assembly lines in about April 1941. The markings of this regiment are discussed further on page 18 of the Camouflage & Markings section.